TITUS
and
PHILEMON

TITUS
and
PHILEMON

by

D. EDMOND HIEBERT

MOODY PRESS

CHICAGO

Printed in the United States of America

CONTENTS

THE EPISTLE TO TITUS

THE EPISTLE TO PHILEMON

THE EPISTLE TO TITUS

An Introduction to Titus

THE TWO LETTERS to Timothy and that to Titus consti-
tute the fourth and last group among the Pauline
Epistles. For more than two centuries they have commonly
been designated as the "Pastoral Epistles." The term is con-
venient, but the modern implications of the term must not
lead us to a misinterpretation of the position of the men
to whom these letters are addressed. Timothy was not the
pastor of the church at Ephesus in the modern sense of that
term; nor was Titus the bishop of the Cretan churches, as
is sometimes thought. Both men are addressed as the personal representatives of the apostle Paul and had been
left at their stations to carry out the work assigned to
them by the apostle. The presence of Titus on Crete did
not alter the local organization and leadership of the
Cretan churches. His work may perhaps be likened to
that of a modern superintendent of missions appointed
over a group of native churches to supervise and strengthen
their organization and spiritual growth.

I Timothy and Titus are companion epistles. Both were
written to men who at the time of writing stood in positions of important ecclesiastical responsibility. That they
were written fairly close together seems obvious. Both
give prominent consideration to matters of ecclesiastical

organization and discipline. Both stress the importance of sound Christian doctrine in the face of prevailing heresy. But the letters show a remarkable difference. I Timothy is more intimate and shows a greater concern for the recipient than does Titus. In I Timothy the emphasis is more on sound doctrine, while in Titus the stress falls on worthy conduct. In Titus Paul insists upon the recognition of the fact that there is an intimate connection between faith and conduct.

The Pauline authorship of the Pastoral Epistles has been under furious attack during the past century and a half. Early external evidence is strongly for it and offers no other view. All critical doubts concerning the Pauline authorship are based entirely on internal and theoretical grounds. The assault has been launched along chronological, ecclesiastical, doctrinal, and linguistic lines. While the subject matter and the linguistic features of these epistles can be used to make quite a case against the conservative position, the arguments are subjective and inconclusive. The conservative position continues to hold the favor of many able scholars and is again receiving wide acceptance in critical circles. We see no compelling reason to abandon the view that they were actually written by Paul, as they claim to be.

Some unsuccessful attempts have been made to fit the Pastoral Epistles into the time of the story of Acts, but it is generally conceded that they must be regarded as belonging to a time following the close of the Book of Acts. The view that Paul was released from the Roman imprisonment of Acts 28 offers the simplest and best solution for the historical data found in these epistles. The Book of Acts is amenable to this view, the Prison Epistles expect it, the Pastoral Epistles demand it, and tradition asserts it. The historical data to be gleaned from these epistles is not full enough to allow us to make a certain reconstruction of the exact course of Paul's journeys following his release from his two-year Roman imprisonment.

The Epistle to Titus indicates that Paul and Titus had labored together on Crete. When Paul had to leave he delegated Titus to remain as his representative to complete the task of organizing and strengthening the churches there. The forthcoming visit of two missionary workers, Zenas and Apollos, offered Paul the immediate opportunity for the writing of the letter. Personal observation of the difficult conditions on Crete, and the realization that Titus would need encouragement and authorization to carry out his assigned task, prompted Paul to write.

The Epistle offers no indication as to where Paul was when he wrote. The place and date assigned to it will vary with one's conjectural reconstruction of Paul's post-Acts ministry. Our view leads us to place the writing of the letter during the first year after Paul's release from prison. We might suggest the time as the fall of A.D. 63, and the place as Corinth.

The purpose of the Epistle must be gleaned from the nature of its contents. A major purpose was to supply Titus with written certification of his authority as the apostolic representative on Crete. The presence on Crete of numerous heretical individuals, who would oppose the work of Titus and question his authority, made the specific authorization desirable. The Epistle was further intended to place in the hands of Titus clear instructions concerning the various phases of his work in the Cretan churches and to urge him to take a positive stand for sound teaching in all the churches.

An Outline of Titus

THE SALUTATION, 1:1-4

    1. The Writer, vv. 1-3
        a. The designation of his position, v. 1a
        b. The nature of his office, v. 1b
        c. The basis of his office, vv. 2, 3a
        d. The function of his office, v. 3b

    2. The Reader, v. 4a

    3. The Greeting, v. 4b

I. CONCERNING ELDERS AND ERRORISTS IN CRETE, 1:5-16

    1. The Appointment of Elders in the Cretan Churches, vv. 5-9
        a. The duties of Titus in Crete, v. 5
        b. The qualification of elders in the congregations, vv. 6-9
            1) The community and domestic qualifications of the elder, v. 6
            2) The personal qualifications of the bishop, vv. 7, 8
            3) The doctrinal qualification of the bishop, v. 9

    2. The Refutation of the False Teachers in Crete, vv. 10-16
        a. The picture of the false teachers, vv. 10-13a
            1) The character of the false teachers, v. 10
            2) The necessity to silence the false teachers, v. 11a

3) The nature of their seductive work, v. 11b
4) The justification for the demand, vv. 12, 13a
   b. The exhortation to the churches in view of the false teachers, vv. 13b, 14
   c. The condemnation of the false teachers, vv. 15, 16
      1) The condemnation from the test of character, v. 15
      2) The condemnation from the test of conduct, v. 16

II. CONCERNING THE NATURAL GROUPS IN THE CONGREGATIONS, 2:1-15
   1. The Instructions to the Groups as to Character and Conduct, vv. 1-10
      a. The duty of Titus properly to instruct the members, v. 1
      b. The instructions relative to various age groups, vv. 2-6
         1) The instructions concerning the old men, v. 2
         2) The instructions concerning the old women, v. 3
         3) The instructions concerning the young women, vv. 4, 5
         4) The instructions concerning the younger men, v. 6
      c. The personal example of Titus, vv. 7, 8
      d. The exhortation to the slaves, vv. 9, 10
         1) The attitude enjoined upon the slaves, v. 9
         2) The conduct of the slaves, vv. 9c, 10a
         3) The motive for such conduct, v. 10b
   2. The Grace of God as the Motive Power for the Christian Life, vv. 11-14
      a. The manifestation of the grace of God, v. 11
      b. The instruction of the grace of God, v. 12

An Outlined Interpretation of Titus

THE SALUTATION, 1:1-4

> Paul, a servant of God, and an apostle of Jesus Christ, according to the faith of God's elect, and the knowledge of the truth which is according to godliness, in hope of eternal life, which God, who cannot lie, promised before times eternal, but in his own seasons manifested his word in the message, wherewith I was intrusted according to the commandment of God our Saviour; to Titus, my true child after a common faith: grace and peace from God the Father and Christ Jesus our Saviour.*

IN KEEPING with the epistolary practice of the day, Paul begins his letter to Titus with a salutation composed of the usual three members; namely, the writer (vv. 1-3), the reader (v. 4a), and the greeting (v. 4b). A writer might expand any one of these to fit the needs of the occasion. Paul's expansion of the first member of the salutation in this letter makes it unusually long for such a brief letter. Its contents are remarkably rich and weighty and are not without difficulty as to their precise interpretation. Paul's descriptive expansion of the first member places the emphasis upon the writer himself and sets forth his official position. But the emphasis is placed, not upon the writer's authority, but upon his duty and the nature of the message he has been commissioned to proclaim. That message is no novelty; it roots back into the eternal past, confidently looks out into the future, and affects present living.

* The text used is that of the American Standard Version (1901).

15

This lengthy preamble is indicative of the purpose of the letter. It was not written to inform Titus of these things concerning the writer. Titus had known these things for years. Paul's primary purpose is not to inform Titus; he is rather thinking of the people with whom Titus is dealing as the apostolic representative. Titus had long been associated with Paul but the people with whom Titus worked on Crete needed to be assured of the true position and message of the apostle whose agent he was. A primary purpose of this letter is to give Titus the needed written authorization for the work which Paul had given him on the island of Crete. Paul was aware that in carrying out his assignment Titus would meet opposition. Circumstances on Crete made it desirable to place in the hands of Titus "written instructions to which he might be able to appeal, whenever the occasion should arise, in proof that he was not acting arbitrarily, but in accordance with positive Apostolic directions" (Van Oosterzee, Introd. to Titus). In this letter the writer, who describes himself and his message at such length, lends his powers to his helper to act for him in the matters contained in it.

1. The Writer, vv. 1-3

That Paul opens the letter with his own name is in accord with the practice of his day. The name "Paul" is from the Latin *Paulus,* meaning *little.* His Hebrew name was "Saul." As a Roman citizen, he probably carried both names from birth. As the apostle to the Gentiles he always uses his Gentile name in his epistles.

The first three verses are used to describe the writer. He designates his position (v. 1a), points out the nature of his office (v. 1b), indicates the basis for his work (vv. 2, 3a), and states the function of his office (v. 3b).

a. The designation of his position, v. 1a. He gives a twofold designation of the writer's position. He is "a servant of God and an apostle of Jesus Christ."

This is the only place where Paul calls himself "a servant *of God*." Elsewhere he uses the expression "a servant of Jesus Christ" (Rom. 1:1; Gal. 1:10; Phil. 1:1). The phrase is used by James and Jude in the salutations of their epistles, and in Revelation 15:3 it is used of Moses. This designation places Paul on a level with Moses and other Old Testament leaders as the servant of Jehovah God. He is God's servant and has been commissioned by Him.

The Greek word *doulos,* here translated "servant," means bondservant or slave. In common usage it carried with it all the unsavory implications of our own word slave. Paul's application of it to himself speaks of his humility and his clear recognition of his true position before God. But Paul is not using the term to imply "involuntary servitude." His use of the term does not exclude the element of free will. A slave is a person who does not regulate his life according to his own will but according to the will of his master. His will has been wholly surrendered to do his master's will. But Paul's surrender was not forced; it was a voluntary surrender of his will to the Lord. When on the Damascus road Paul came face to face with the Lord, his first question, indicative of his attitude of submission, was, "Who art thou, Lord?" (Acts 9:5). No one ever becomes a successful servant of God until he chooses to make God's will his own will. Paul's will was not crushed but he imbibed the will of his Master as his own. Do we profess to be servants of God yet continue to insist on carrying out our own will for our lives?

A slave does not own himself but is owned by his master. Paul recognized that he was not his own but that he belonged to God to serve Him and to further His work. As Christians we have been bought with a great price, the precious blood of Christ (I Cor. 6:19, 20; I Peter 1:18, 19), hence we are not our own but belong to Him. This lays upon believers the obligation "that they that live should no longer live unto themselves, but unto him who for their sakes died and rose again" (II Cor. 5:15). This was the spirit that motivated the labors of Paul. It is this spirit that is so tragically lacking among Christians today.

Paul further designates his position by calling himself "an apostle of Jesus Christ." The first designation was general, indicating his personal relationship to God; this is specific, indicating his official relationship to Jesus Christ. The Greek word here translated "and" (*de*) adds something that is different. As the apostle of Jesus Christ he belongs to a distinct class of people. Like the Twelve, he has been called and commissioned by Jesus Christ as His messenger. He is Jesus Christ's envoy or ambassador, sent to represent Him and His revelation.

A few unimportant manuscripts here have the order "Christ Jesus" instead of "Jesus Christ." Both orders are used by Paul in each group of his epistles, but the order "Christ Jesus" is more frequent in the later epistles. The average English reader uses either order merely to identify the Person to whom reference is being made. But to Paul and his Greek readers each order had its own significance. In each case the first member of the compound name indicates whether the theological or the historical idea concerning our Lord is chiefly in the writer's mind. The word "Christ" comes from the Greek word *christos* and is the equivalent of the Hebrew word translated "Messiah." Both words mean "the anointed one." On the opening pages of the Gospels "the Christ" is not a personal name but an official designation meaning the Messiah (cf. Matt. 2:4); only later as Jesus became positively accepted as the Messiah by His followers did it become a personal name. The term thus speaks of His Messianic dignity, the fact that He is the fulfillment of the Old Testament promises concerning the coming Messiah. The name "Jesus" comes from the Greek *Iēsous,* which in turn comes from the Hebrew name "Jehoshua" or "Joshua" which means "Jehovah saves." It was the name given Him by the angel before His birth (Luke 1:31; Matt. 1:21). It speaks of the fact of the Incarnation and is His human name. The compound name "Christ Jesus" emphasizes the theological fact that the One who was with the Father in eternal glory became incarnate in human form. The order "Jesus Christ" places the emphasis on the historical appearing of the man Jesus, who by faith was recognized and acknowledged as the Christ of God. It speaks of One who humbled Himself, became obedient unto death, but was afterward exalted and glorified. This order of the compound name connects Paul's apostleship with the new revelation of God made in the crucified and risen Lord.

The two references to Deity, "a servant of God, and an apostle of Jesus Christ," indicate two aspects of Paul's relationship to the Divine: he is a servant of the Supreme Being known to the fathers, and also His apostle as He revealed Himself in the sphere of human history in Jesus Christ.

b. The nature of his office, v. 1b. The nature of his apostolic office is asserted to be "according to the faith of God's elect, and the knowledge of the truth which is according to godliness." His office is defined in relation to two facts of spiritual experience—"faith" and "knowledge."

The original expression here rendered "according to the faith" (*kata pistin*) has been differently interpreted. Many scholars understand it as a statement of the object or purpose of Paul's apostleship. They would render it "*with regard to,* or *for,* the faith of God's elect." When this is interpreted to mean that the object of his apostleship was "to produce faith" in God's elect, it conflicts with the New Testament usage of the term "God's elect." In the New Testament it "is always used of those who have already become believers, never of those who have not yet received the call" (Huther). Others broaden the thought by suggesting that the aim of Paul's apostleship was "to bring about, cherish, and perfect" the faith of the elect (Alford). That Paul's apostolic labors had this as their aim is obvious.

But the translation *"for* the faith of God's elect" seems too wide a departure from the ordinary meaning of the Greek. It naturally means "according to the faith." This rendering is possible in each of the four instances that the word (*kata*) occurs in this salutation; but it cannot be consistently rendered "for" or "with a view to" in each instance. The translation "according to the faith" is rejected by many scholars on the ground that it would describe Paul's message as in some way regulated by the faith of the elect, a thing which Paul denied (Gal. 1:1-5). But the difficulty vanishes when we remember that Paul is defining his apostleship as being in accord with the new revelation in Jesus Christ to which the elect have responded. There is perfect harmony between what Paul is and what God's elect have, namely, their faith and knowledge. When false teachers attack and deny his apostleship they reveal that they do not have the true faith but are following a spurious teaching.

The teaching concerning "the elect of God" is surrounded with mystery and has been the subject of not a little controversy. God does have His elect whom He Himself chose in eternity (Eph. 1:4; II Tim. 1:9). But this choice in no way removes our responsibility as free moral agents. The doctrine is for believers, and Paul intended it to be practical. It bids the believer, who at the invitation of the Gospel rests upon Christ and His grace and is thus assured of his salvation, to look back and upward "in order that he may find the beginning and ground of this unspeakable salvation, not in anything in himself, but solely in the free mercy of the electing counsel of God" (*Lange Commentary*). It is intended as a comfort to the faithful, struggling man of God, for it tells him the eternal God chose him "before the foundation of the world" to be His servant.

Paul further describes his apostleship as being in accord with "the knowledge of the truth which is according to godliness." It is in entire agreement with a full inner apprehension of the divine truth as presented in the evangelical message. The Christian is not dependent upon some "uncertain, vague, speculative knowledge, like that of the various sects of philosophers" (Boise). In Christ he possesses the advanced knowledge (*epignōsin*) of a matured spiritual life.

The truth which the believer has come to realize is described by an attributive phrase as being "according to godliness." There is an intimate connection between truth and godliness. A vital possession of truth is inconsistent with irreverence. "The so-called truths of philosophy and science were then, as they are now, often far removed from reverence and piety" (Boise). But real truth never deviates from the path of piety. A profession of the truth which allows an individual to live in ungodliness is a spurious profession. "The objective truth and the subjective godliness correspond, and this correspondence is the criterion of the genuineness of both" (Riggenbach, quoted in Horton).

c. The basis of his office, vv. 2, 3a. Paul points out that his apostolic office is based on the hope of eternal life, and then he indicates that this eternal life is grounded in the past promise of God and has received a present manifestation in the Gospel.

The expression "in hope of eternal life" is quite literally, "resting on hope of eternal life" (*ep' elpidi zōēs aioniou*). The connection of the clause is not quite certain. Some would relate it directly to the statement about the faith and knowledge of the elect just preceding, thus making it a general description of the Christian life. More probably it is to be connected with the entire preceding statement describing the nature of Paul's apostolic office. The hope of eternal life is the sure foundation upon which the apostolic calling rests. This is the hope in which Paul cheerfully endures his toil and sufferings.

"Eternal life" is the present possession of all who put their faith in the Son of God (John 3:36; I John 5:11, 12). But here the idea of futurity is the prominent thought, since it is spoken of as the "hope" of eternal life. Only those who possess eternal life here and now can truly have the hope of this future life. It anticipates the consummation of the Christian hope at the return of our Lord Jesus Christ. This is the glorious climax toward which the Christian life moves and for which the true believer eagerly waits.

The remainder of verse two and the first part of verse three describe this eternal life. It is grounded in God's past promise and has been manifested in the Gospel.

This life was the subject of divine promise. "Which [life] God, who cannot lie, promised before times eternal." The hope is sure because the realization of the promise rests upon the character of God. He is the God "who cannot lie" (literally, "the un-lie-able God"). He is the absolutely faithful and true God; His promise is sure of fulfillment.

And this "eternal life," Paul says, God promised "before times eternal." Interpretations differ as to the meaning of "before times eternal." Some understand Paul to mean simply "from ancient times," that is, the Old Testament ages reaching as far back as Adam. But in the light of Paul's statement in II Timothy 1:9, it seems best to view these words as reaching back into eternity past. It is sometimes asserted that no such promise was made until after the creation of man. To this Boise replies: "May not the promise have been made to the Son, the future Redeemer, in eternity? The purpose and the promise were naturally coeval." The difficulty is removed when we regard the statement as a mixed one. In his thought the apostle mingles the fact of the eternal purpose of God toward man with the actual announcement of it in time, for the historical announcement concerning eternal life sprang out of the eternal purpose.

This promise of eternal life God brought to manifestation in history in the message of the Gospel. The manifestation He made "in his own seasons," that is, the appropriate seasons determined by God in His own wisdom. Says Lock: "The thought of the Incarnation taking place at the right moment in the world's history is a favorite one with St. Paul (Gal. 4:4; Rom. 5:6; Eph. 1:10; Acts 17:26)." By "his *word*" Paul does not mean the Incarnate Word, Jesus Christ, as some ancient as well as modern interpreters have thought. It has reference rather to the Gospel in which the promise was embodied. And this word, in turn, was announced through the instrumentality of the "message" proclaimed. The original word (*kērugma*) denotes not so much the act of preaching as the content of the proclamation of the herald. The picture is that of a herald or public crier making an official announcement.

d. The function of his office, v. 3b. The thought of the proclamation of the promise of God in the Gospel message leads Paul at once to speak of his own relation to that Gospel. His function as Christ's apostle is to herald the message of eternal life. For Paul the preaching of the Gospel was not a self-chosen occupation. It was a trust divinely committed to him which he could not escape. (This is made emphatic in the original by the transposition of the verb and the subject and the use of the emphatic pronoun I). Paul never got away from his sense of being divinely commissioned as a messenger of the Gospel. Failure to carry out this trust would have been culpable. "Woe is unto me, if I preach not the gospel"

(I Cor. 9:16). How God's servants need this sense of inescapable responsibility today!

This entrustment with the life-giving message was made to Paul "according to the commandment of God our Saviour." A special order from God conveyed this trust to him. And the trust was given to him by "God our Saviour." The reference is to God the Father. The title "Saviour" Paul applies to God the Father six times in the Pastoral Epistles (I Tim. 1:1; 2:3; 4:10; Titus 1:3; 2:10; 3:4). He does not use the term of God the Father outside the Pastorals, although the thought is found in I Corinthians 1:21. (See also Luke 1:47; Jude 25.) Elsewhere Paul presents his commission as being given by Christ (Gal. 1:12), but here he refers it directly to God the Father since his commission is intimately related to the promise of life which God Himself had promised. Since the Father is the ultimate source and fount of all human salvation this title is appropriately applied to Him. The personal pronoun "our" speaks of personal appropriation and confession of Him before men. He is the Saviour of all who accept and confess Him.

2. The Reader, v. 4a

The second and third members of the salutation are brief. The reader is named and briefly described. "To Titus, my true child after a common faith."

The personal references to Titus are comparatively few in this Epistle, but such references as occur are consistent with what we learn about him elsewhere. Although he was an intimate associate of Paul, the name of Titus never occurs in the Book of Acts. Only in the Pauline Epistles does his name occur, nine of the thirteen occurrences of his name being in II Corinthians.

From Galatians 2:3 we learn that Titus was a Greek. Paul took him along to the Jerusalem Conference as a test case for the validity of his Gospel. The demand for his circumcision by the Judaizers was successfully resisted and Paul's position was confirmed (Gal. 2:1-5).

We first learn of Titus as an active assistant to Paul while Paul was laboring at Ephesus during the third missionary journey. Titus was sent as Paul's envoy to the church at Corinth. Apparently from Ephesus Paul sent him to Corinth to initiate the project of the offering for the Judean saints (II Cor. 8:6, 10). Following the writing of our I Corinthians, Paul again sent Titus to Corinth to take a hand in straightening out the tangled affairs in that church. Their plans called for Titus to return to Paul at Troas. The continued absence of Titus caused Paul great concern about the state of affairs at Corinth, so, in order the sooner to meet Titus, he left Troas and went into Macedonia. Here Titus met him with the cheering news of the successful completion of his mission (II Cor. 2:12, 13; 7:5-7). In response to the report of Titus, Paul wrote our II Corinthians and sent Titus back with it to Corinth and commissioned him to complete the offering begun in Corinth a year before (II Cor. 8:6, 16-24).

The ability of Titus successfully to deal with the thorny situation in the Corinthian church reveals him to be a man of insight, tact, and effective spiritual leadership. Paul's references to Titus in II Corinthians show the high esteem in which Paul held him. "He is a trustworthy, confidential delegate, walking in the Apostle's steps, walking in the same spirit (II Cor. 12:18), his 'brother' (II Cor. 2:13), his fellow worker and sharer of his toils (8:23)" (Lock).

Our knowledge concerning the further activities of Titus is left blank until we come to this Epistle addressed to Titus while he was working on Crete. Our last glimpse of Titus is contained in II Timothy, written during Paul's second Roman imprisonment. Titus has been with Paul in Rome but has gone to Dalmatia, evidently on an evangelistic errand for the apostle (II Tim. 4:10).

Paul addresses Titus as "my true child after a common faith." The expression implies that Paul has been instrumental in the conversion of Titus; but we have no further information on the matter. The employment of the term "child" indicates dearness, while the adjective "true" or "genuine" is an acknowledgment that Titus is running true to his spiritual parentage. Titus is his true child "according to a common faith." Their relationship is in the realm of their "common faith." It is their mutually held faith that places them into accord with one another and with all the elect who share this faith. Some have thought that Paul has in mind the original difference between himself and Titus, he being a Jewish Christian, and Titus a Gentile Christian, but there is nothing in the statement to indicate that thought.

3. The Greeting, v. 4b.

The greeting is similar to that found in Paul's other epistles. "Grace and peace from God the Father and Christ Jesus our Saviour." Manuscript authority is against the insertion of the term "mercy" found in the King James Version. Critical editions of the Greek text omit it. It rightly appears in both of the letters to Timothy.

The form of the greeting is distinctively Christian. It is possible that the form was originated by Paul. The form of address most usual in a Greek letter of the time may be seen in Acts 15:23; 23:26; James 1:1. The commonplace "greeting" Paul replaces with a statement indicative of the heart of the Christian faith. It mentions both the nature of the desired blessings and the source to which he looks for their bestowal.

He desires "grace and peace" for Titus. "Grace" is the divine love manifesting itself toward guilty sinners in free forgiveness and unmerited blessing. It speaks of our own unworthiness and the spontaneous redeeming act of God in Christ when there was nothing in us to merit it. "Peace" is the resultant reconciliation experienced by those who respond to the grace of God. It is the outcome of the restoration of harmony between our soul and God on the basis of the atonement. Our hearts are kept in peace as we realize that the unmerited favor of God has been bestowed upon us in Christ.

This twofold blessing Paul thinks of as coming "from God the Father and Christ Jesus our Saviour." Both are involved in the bestowal of "grace and peace." The ultimate source is God the Father who devised our salvation in the sending of His Son, while the immediate source is "Christ Jesus our Saviour," through whose atoning work grace and peace become freely available to all through faith. In verse three the epithet "Saviour" was applied to the Father; here it is applied to Christ Jesus. This is the only place where the term is used of Christ in a salutation, although the term is common elsewhere. (In the Pastoral Epistles it is used of the Father six times, and four times of the Son.) Both Father and Son are our Saviour, for the salvation which they bestow is the same. This double use of the term Saviour is clear proof of Paul's conviction of the true deity of Christ Jesus.

In view of the brevity of the epistle itself, the length and profundity of the salutation are remarkable. It offers a strong argument in favor of the genuineness of the epistle. It has all the most characteristic ideas of Paul's teaching in it, yet contains a number of distinctive features which speak of the originality of the writer. It is hard to believe that it could be a literary forgery as the critics claim. Horton well says: "A forger may imitate his original with servility, or he may strike into gross divergencies; but it is almost beyond the reach of art to be so different that copying is out of the question, and yet so like that the personal characteristics of the original are unmistakable."

The body of the Epistle falls into three main divisions, corresponding to our chapter divisions. The first division

(1:5-16) is concerned with the proper organization of the churches on Crete, which is necessary because of the presence of numerous false teachers. In chapter two, which forms the second division, Paul deals with the various groups in the congregations and urges upon them a becoming Christian conduct. The third division (3:1-11) is wider in its scope and sets forth the duty of believers among men generally.

I. CONCERNING ELDERS AND ERRORISTS IN CRETE, 1:5-16

This first division naturally divides into two sections. Verses 5-9 relate to the appointment of elders in the churches, while verses 10-16 deal with the necessary refutation of the false teachers in Crete.

1. The Appointment of Elders in the Cretan Churches, vv. 5-9

> For this cause left I thee in Crete, that thou shouldest set in order the things that were wanting, and appoint elders in every city, as I gave thee charge; if any man is blameless, the husband of one wife, having children that believe, who are not accused of riot or unruly. For the bishop must be blameless, as God's steward; not self-willed, not soon angry, no brawler, no striker, not greedy of filthy lucre; but given to hospitality, a lover of good, sober-minded, just, holy, self-controlled; holding to the faithful word which is according to the teaching, that he may be able both to exhort in the sound doctrine, and to convict the gainsayers.

Following the salutation the Epistle at once assumes a practical character. In the elaborate salutation Paul has stamped all the acts of Titus with his own name and authority. That authority must now be used by Titus in his further work of ordering affairs in the Cretan churches. He is reminded of the duties that have been placed on him (v. 5), and is then given a detailed delineation of the moral qualifications of the men to be appointed as elders (vv. 6-9).

a. The duties of Titus in Crete, v. 5. This verse gives us the historical setting for the Epistle. Titus is working on the island of Crete when Paul writes to him. Crete is one of the largest islands in the Mediterranean, situated almost equidistant from Europe, Asia, and Africa. A high state of civilization once flourished there, but by New Testament times the moral level of its inhabitants was deplorable. Their ferocity and fraud were widely attested; their falsehood was proverbial; the wine of Crete was famous, and drunkenness prevailed.

As indicated in Paul's words, Paul had worked with Titus on Crete. The Book of Acts does not make any mention of Paul working there. Paul's brief stay at Fair Havens on Crete while on his way to Rome as a prisoner cannot be the time mentioned here. Nor was Titus with him at that time. The varied attempts to fit the travels of Paul, mentioned in the Pastoral Epistles, into the Acts story are unsatisfactory. Paul's work on Crete clearly belongs to the period of his activities after the first Roman imprisonment.

Just how long Paul worked with Titus on Crete is not known, but apparently it was not long before the demand for his presence elsewhere compelled him to depart, leaving Titus behind to carry on the work that still remained to be done. The compound form of the verb translated "left" (*apelipon*) implies that the being left behind was temporary, rather than permanent. Accordingly White remarks: "St. Paul's language favors the supposition that the commission given to Titus was that of a temporary apostolic legate rather than of a permanent local president." That Titus was not the permanent bishop on Crete is evident from 3:12, where Paul speaks of sending another worker to replace him.

Paul indicates the duties placed upon Titus in the

words: "For this cause left I thee in Crete, that thou shouldest set in order the things that were wanting, and appoint elders in every city." The comprehensive duty was to "set in order the things that were wanting." The verb rendered "set in order" (*epidiorthōsē*) means "to further set in order, to further set straight." It implies that Paul had begun the work of setting in order the things that were wanting, and now Titus is to continue that work. The word was used by medical writers of setting broken bones or straightening out crooked ones. There is accordingly no basis for the supposition that Paul himself had planted Christianity on Crete. Just when Christianity was introduced there we do not know. The whole tenor of the Epistle implies that Christianity was widespread on Crete and had been in existence long enough to admit irregularities, and to be endangered by false teachers. The churches were deficient in organization and needed positive instruction in doctrine and Christian living. With these needs Titus is to deal. And what a task he had! As Green says: "Setting in order churches that have gone wrong is a delicate and large task—more difficult in many ways than evangelizing new fields. False teachings are hard to correct, and when sin gets into a church, it is difficult to dislodge it."

"And appoint elders in every city." The "and" introduces an additional and emphatic particular which required attention. These Christian assemblies were without sufficient organization and lacked effective leadership. This lack Titus must remedy. In city by city on the island where there were groups of believers he is to "appoint elders." The rendering "appoint" is better than the rendering "ordain" in the King James Version, since it avoids the tendency to read the modern technical meaning of that word into the situation. The verb quite literally means "to set down," hence "to appoint one to administer an office." The method of selection of these elders is not fixed by the word. It does seem to mark the responsible part which Titus took in the affair. Apparently the selection was made by the whole assembly under the guidance of Titus; then those selected were formally appointed to office under the leadership of Titus. This was to be done "in every city." Says Harvey: "Here was no diocesan episcopacy, but the church in every city has its own body of elders."

By the added phrase, "as I gave thee charge," Paul indicates that the commission being given to Titus had already been given him by word of mouth. When Paul left he had communicated his duties to Titus orally; now this letter formally invests him with the authority to act as Paul's agent in the work.

b. The qualifications of elders in the congregations, vv. 6-9. It was imperative for the cause of Christianity that the right type of men be placed in positions of leadership in the Cretan churches. Paul's enumeration of the necessary qualifications falls into three groups: the elder's social and domestic relationships (v. 6), his personal qualifications (vv. 7, 8), and his doctrinal qualification (v. 9).

1) The community and domestic qualifications of the elder, v. 6. The first of the three qualifications listed in verse 6 is general and relates to the community standing of the man. He must be "blameless," that is, "unaccused." He must have nothing laid to his charge. He must be a man about whose past or present accusations are not being circulated.

The next two items deal with his domestic qualifications. "The husband of one wife." Three views have been taken of this much discussed requirement: (1) that he must be married; (2) that he must not remarry if his first wife dies; (3) that he must not have more than one living wife at a time. The first of these cannot be meant since Paul says "one" not "a" wife. However the statement does imply that in apostolic churches the elders were married men and consequently rules out the Roman Catholic dogma of the celibacy of the clergy. The second view, having the sanction of noted expositors, both ancient and modern, is highly improbable in view of Paul's clear teaching concerning second marriages (I Tim. 5:14; Rom. 7:2-3; I Cor. 7:39). We hold to the third view. Paul is insisting upon the inviolable sanctity of the marriage relationship. In view of the loose divorce practices then prevalent among the Romans as well as the Jews, as also the practice of polygamy, the restriction was timely for the influence of the church.

Since the elders would be chosen from men of maturity it is taken for granted that he would be the head of a family. "Having children that believe, who are not accused of riot or unruly." The original (*pista*) may mean either "trustworthy" or "believing" children. Evidently the latter is intended here. The elder's children must also be Christians. If he is not able to win his own children to the faith, how will he lead others to the faith? "The family is the nursery of the church and these two act and react upon each other so that a bad or weak father can never be an efficient elder" (Lipscomb). The children must live restrained and disciplined lives. They must not be accused of being dissolute or profligate, like the prodigal son. Nor must they be accused of a refusal to bow to parental authority. "Inability to train and govern a family creates a presumption of inability to train and govern the church" (Harvey).

2) The personal qualifications of the bishop, vv. 7, 8. "The bishop must be blameless." The article does not refer to an individual person but to the class. Here is clear evidence that the designations "elder" and "bishop" were used to refer to the same person, since "bishop" here evidently refers to the "elder" of verse 5. All official distinctions between bishop and elder, elevating the one above the other, are of post-apostolic origin and foreign

to Scripture. The two designations refer to the same person, yet with a difference in connotation. The term "elder" (*presbuteros*), derived from Jewish usage, emphasizes the personal dignity and maturity of the individual holding the office; the term "bishop" (*episkopos*), coming from the Greek, points to the function of the officer as that of an overseer. Here, where the emphasis upon the office rather than the man is prominent, the official term is appropriate.

"As God's steward" the officer must be blameless. Because of his position he is a manager or administrator of God's house, dispensing under God to the members of the household the mysteries of God (I Cor. 4:1) and His manifold grace (I Peter 4:10). He is *"God's* steward" (emphatic by position) and is therefore directly accountable to Him. This requires of him a conformity to the highest moral and spiritual qualifications.

Five negative qualities are first listed (v. 7b), pointing out the qualities which the model bishop should not have. (1) "Not self-willed," not having a self-loving spirit which seeks to gratify self in arrogant disregard of others. (2) "Not soon angry," not quick-tempered, easily flaring up in anger; not having his temper under control. (3) "No brawler." The compound form used here (*paroinos*) quite literally means "one who sits alongside of wine"; then it came to have a secondary meaning, one addicted to wine, and hence acting under the influence of wine. Wine was clearly recognized as an evil and the bishop must avoid it. The word, if not absolutely prohibitory of wine, certainly requires strict temperance in the use of it. Ernest Gordon, translating it literally as "not present at wine," says it means that the bishop must not be "in drinking-places or parties."[1] (4) "No striker," not quick with his fists, not given to acts of bodily violence. "A man who

1 Ernest Gordon, *Christ, the Apostles, and Wine. An Exegetical Study* (1944), p. 35. (Sunday School Times Co.).

might involve himself in a street brawl would soon bring the Church into disrespect" (Scott). A certain pastor got into an argument with his deacon and in the heated argument knocked the deacon down, and thereby he knocked himself out of his church and all influence in the community. (5) "Not greedy of filthy lucre." The word quite literally means "not eager for shameful gain." He is not to use his office as a means for the accumulation of unjust gain. Our striking English rendering "filthy lucre" is at times, wrongly so, made to imply that money itself, fees, or other material gains in themselves are worldly and unfit to be sought for by any minister who professes to set an example as a spiritual leader. It has been well said: " 'Fair gains' are the parson's right for fair pains" (Humphreys). The laborer is worthy of his hire, but the ministry must not be considered a money-making business. If the minister's mind is simply occupied with the amassing of gold he will be too preoccupied to feed the flock.

These negative qualifications Paul supplements with six positive characteristics which the bishop must manifest (v. 8). (1) "Given to hospitality," that is, devoted to or a lover of hospitality. He should be one who gladly opened his home to entertain strangers or the needy. The conditions of the times made such hospitality on the part of Christians very important. Believers in their travels could not resort to the homes of heathen or to the public inns without being exposed to insult and danger. It was important that fellow believers offer them hospitality on their way. It was further necessary because Christians were often persecuted and rendered homeless. But it may well be that Paul has in mind that "broader signification, so beautifully worded in the Epistle to the Hebrews, where we are told not to be forgetful to entertain *strangers*, for thereby some have entertained angels unawares (Heb. 13:2)" (Spence). (2) "A lover of good." The Greek form rendered "good" may mean either "good things" or "good persons." The former is wider and seems preferable. The bishop is to be a man who is devoted to that which is good or beneficial, whether in men, deeds, or things. (3) "Sober-minded," not light and frivolous, but serious, discreet, and sober in deportment. He is to be self-controlled and balanced in his opinions and actions. (4) "Just," upright in his dealings with men. His conduct in relation to others must conform to the standard of right. Any minister who is not upright in all his dealings with his fellow men can do little good. (5) "Holy" (*hosios*) is not the ordinary word translated holy. This word means pure, unpolluted, free from the stain of sin. It speaks of the individual who keeps himself free from that which stains him in the eyes of God. It has been pointed out that the last three words present the three sides of human duty—duty to one's self, duty to one's neighbor, and duty toward God. (6) "Self-controlled" means literally "one in control of strength." He has the power to control all his desires and appetites, is temporate in all things. A sober-minded man is moderate in the enjoyment of what is lawful; the self-controlled man refrains from all that is unlawful and harmful.

3) The doctrinal qualification of the bishop, v. 9. As the leader in the church the bishop must be true to the faith of the church. The statement of the doctrinal qualification reads, "holding to the faithful word which is according to the teaching." He must continue to cling to the faithful word and that in the face of opposition and temptation to abandon it. He must not be "tossed to and fro and carried about with every wind of doctrine" (Eph. 4:14). He must be characterized by doctrinal stability. He clings to the "faithful word" because he knows it to be trustworthy and dependable, not unreliable and treacherous like the spurious teachings of the false teachers. This Word is more precisely defined as being "according to

the teaching." It is in full agreement with the teaching
given by the apostles. The statement presupposes the
existence of a body of Christian teaching which, in substance if not in form, was already fixed. To this Word,
reliable and worthy of utmost confidence, the bishop
must resolutely cling if he is to fulfill his function.

The reason for the doctrinal qualification is "that he
may be able both to exhort in the sound doctrine, and to
convict the gainsayers." His work as bishop relates both to
the members of the flock and to the enemies of the flock.
"The shepherd must be able to tend the sheep, and to
drive away wolves" (White). In reference to believers his
work is "to exhort in the sound doctrine." His exhortation
is to admonish, encourage, and strengthen them. The
"doctrine" is the field or sphere in which his exhortation
is to find its topics. It is wonderfully adapted to build up
the believer in his spiritual life. The doctrine is described
as being "*sound* doctrine," a phrase peculiar to the Pastoral Epistles. The word means "healthful" teaching, and
so stands in direct contrast to the sickly, morbid, and
unpractical teaching of the false teachers. But who wants
unhealthy or diseased doctrine? People are very particular
about getting healthful food for the physical body, yet,
sadly enough, seem quite unconcerned when they are
fed diseased and death-producing doctrine from the pulpit. The validity and power of the minister's exhortation
lies in its conformity to the great verities of the Christian
revelation.

But the bishop must also deal with the opponents of
the truth. "The gainsayers," those who speak against and
oppose the sound doctrine, it is his duty "to convict." The
word means more than reprove; it signifies a presentation
of evidence so that the arguments of the opponents are
beaten down and proved to be baseless. Hence Bernard
well remarks: "A firm grasp of the truth is the indis-

pensable preparation for him who would undertake to dispel error."

It is to be noted that nothing directly is said about the work of the elders. The emphasis is rather upon the character of the men placed in charge of the work. If the church gets such ministers the work will prosper. The church must appoint such men if it is to remain true to its mission and resist the assaults of doctrinal apostasy and open ungodliness. These qualifications outline the ideal toward which each local assembly must look in the selection of its minister. Are we insisting strongly enough on these qualifications for our ministers? Do we refuse men who do not have them? In admitting a man to the ministry the primary consideration must ever be the integrity of his character rather than his spectacular gifts. "No intellectual power or pulpit brilliancy can atone for the lack of solid Christian virtues and a blameless life" (Harvey).

2. The Refutation of the False Teachers in Crete, vv. 10-16

For there are many unruly men, vain talkers and deceivers, specially they of the circumcision, whose mouths must be stopped; men who overthrow whole houses, teaching things which they ought not, for filthy lucre's sake. One of themselves, a prophet of their own, said, Cretans are always liars, evil beasts, idle gluttons. This testimony is true. For which cause reprove them sharply, that they may be sound in the faith, not giving heed to Jewish fables, and commandments of men who turn away from the truth. To the pure all things are pure: but to them that are defiled and unbelieving nothing is pure: but both their mind and their conscience are defiled. They profess that they know God; but by their works they deny him, being abominable, and disobedient, and unto every good work reprobate.

The opening "for" connects this paragraph with what has just been said. The insistence upon the qualification that the bishop be able to convict gainsayers is justified in view of the numerous heretics in Crete. The situation there shows how proper this requirement is. He will have ample occasion to encounter such adversaries. Paul now proceeds to describe more particularly the chief opponents Titus will be dealing with in his work.

This section may be divided into three parts: the picture of the false teachers (vv. 10-13a), the exhortation to the churches in view of the false teachers (vv. 13b, 14), and the evidence condemning the false teachers (vv. 15, 16).

a. The picture of the false teachers, vv. 10-13a. A faithful portrayal of these men affords a lurid picture indeed. With a few deft strokes Paul sketches their character (v. 10), demands that they be silenced (v. 11a), describes the nature of their seductive work (v. 11b), and quotes from a Cretan prophet as justification for the demand (vv. 12, 13a).

The gainsayers of verse 9 are not strictly to be equated with these false teachers. These men form a special class among them, the most pernicious of the opponents, and they must be dealt with in a special way. That they were not heathen but professed Christians is obvious not only from their profession (v. 16), but also from the tragic success of their deceptive penetration into Christian households (v. 11). They were teachers, primarily of Jewish background, who pandered in their teaching to the corrupt inclinations in people, dwelt upon Jewish legends of the patriarchs (compare the scroll on Genesis among the recently discovered Dead Sea Scrolls), apparently professed to have some higher revelations for the religious life which they presented as a higher philosophy, and accompanied their doctrines with prescriptions of certain ritual observances to which they attached great moral and social value.

Many scholars take for granted that these men were recognized members of the Christian churches on Crete. But this seems doubtful. It is difficult to conceive that any members of the church would deliberately practice such deception as is spoken of here. The difficulty is further increased by the statement that they were primarily of the circumcision. Since no mention is made of any insistence upon the rite of circumcision, it seems obvious that they were not the type of Judaizers whom Paul denounced in Galatians. Their teaching seems to be similar to the heretical teaching which was seeking to invade the Colossian church. These teachers seem to have definite affinities to the teachers Timothy is to resist in I Timothy. As professed Christians they kept alongside of the work of the church and exhibited some affinities with it, and by their deceptive methods sought to gain a following within the churches, but they were not a true part of it.

1) The character of the false teachers, v 10. "There are many unruly men." The word "many" enumerates this pernicious group. The sad fact that they are numerous makes them all the more dangerous. Three terms are employed to describe them. "Unruly." They are characterized as men who refuse to submit to control. Although professing to be Christians they set themselves up in opposition to the Gospel and refuse to be obedient to it. "Vain talkers." They are adept at fluent and appealing speech but their talk leads to no constructive good. "Deceivers." They are deceivers of men's minds, as the original implies. Their teaching has a seductive and perilous fascination over the minds of its victims, deceiving them and leading them astray.

In the added words, "specially they of the circumcision," Paul points out the chief source of origin of this teaching. Although they profess to be converts to Christianity, their teaching stems largely from Judaism and deals with things Jewish. Josephus and others inform us that there were many Jews on the island of Crete.

2) The necessity to silence the false teachers, v. 11a. "Whose mouths must be stopped." Titus is informed in plain language that these men must not be tolerated. They must be silenced. The word is a stronger one than that used in reference to the gainsayers in verse 9. It literally means "to put something into the mouth," and was used both of a bridle and a muzzle. The latter seems preferable here, since the word often means to reduce to silence. Like dangerous beasts these men needed to be muzzled. How that was to be done Paul does not say. Perhaps when they sought to get a public hearing for their doctrines in the assembly they were to be forbidden to talk, not be given an opportunity to use their deceptive speech on the people. A more effective way to gag them would be to use the truth on them, as our Lord silenced the Sadducees (Matt. 22:34) by holding up the truth before them so decidedly and powerfully that no further opposition was possible.

3) The nature of their seductive work, v. 11b. Vigorous action against them was necessary because of the evil nature of their work. The effect of their work was deplorable. They belonged to a class of men who "overthrow whole houses." These disastrous effects they were producing by means of their false doctrines and deceptive declarations. Entire families were disturbed and turned topsy-turvy. Having gained entry into individual Christian homes and subverted their faith, they sought to use these members to secure a following in the assembly. And the motivating force behind their vicious work was "for filthy lucre's sake." A mercenary motive, rather than a fanatical religious zeal, lay behind their efforts. Having surreptitiously gotten into certain families, they traded upon the ignorance, or curiosity, or even vice of the people, extracting money from them in a way which

justifies Paul's strong expression. With this as their aim their teaching naturally accommodated itself to the tastes of the people. The majority of the false teachers would soon stop if their evil work did not produce financial profits.

4) The justification for the demand, vv. 12, 13a. The presence of men of this character working on Crete was bad enough, but to make it worse Paul knew that they were only in harmony with the nature of the people among whom they found their prey. The general character of the Cretans themselves was such as to offer them a ready starting point for their evil work. In confirmation thereof Paul quotes the testimony of a noted native Cretan, "one of themselves"; hence he could quote him without offense. Paul calls him "a prophet." This does not mean that Paul considered him inspired. He uses the term since the Cretans themselves recognized and esteemed him as such.

Paul quotes from Epimenides, a native of Gnossus in Crete. He lived around 600 B.C. (Plato dated him at 500 B.C.) and is described by the ancients as a poet, a priest, and a prophet. Cicero ascribed to him the ability to foresee future events. He is said to have foretold the Persian war ten years before it happened. Many popular legends gathered around him and it is said that even divine honors came to be paid to him.

The testimony of Epimenides, in the form of a hexameter line, is not complimentary to his countrymen. "Cretans are always liars, evil beasts, idle gluttons." This threefold accusation against the Cretans is supported by the evidence of other secular sources. The falsehood of the Cretans was proverbial. The expression "to Cretize" meant "to lie," and "to play the Cretan with a Cretan" meant "to out-trick a trickster." "Evil beasts" testifies to their wild, fierce nature, their ferocity, their love of cruelty. "Idle gluttons" means that they were so governed by gluttony as to have become merely indolent bellies, a burden to their possessor.

Paul adds, "This testimony is true." According to the ancient proverb the Cretans, the Cappadocians, and the Cilicians were the worst three "C's" of antiquity. That Paul should thus confirm this uncomplimentary quotation is striking. Scott cannot believe that the writer would thus insult his Cretan readers. What Paul means is that the words of Epimenides about the Cretans are still true. Of course he does not mean that all the Cretans were liars; there were noble exceptions to this general characterization of the Cretans. But these false teachers, themselves Cretans, are standing examples of it. As Horton points out: "The three characteristics of the Cretans reappear in these false teachers; 'liars,' vain talkers and deceivers of verses 10, 11: 'evil beasts,' unruly and overturning houses; 'idle gluttons,' the base gain, and perhaps the riot and love of wine, which are implicitly condemned in the characteristics of a bishop." But all such things Christianity has come to stop and must be eliminated from the church. Paul faces the facts and deals with them squarely in order that they may be recognized and removed. It is the glory of Christianity that it can lead people such as this to "live soberly, righteously, and godly" (2:12).

b. The exhortation to the churches in view of the false teachers, vv. 13b, 14. "For this cause reprove them sharply." Who are the "them"? Some understand Paul to refer to the false teachers. Rather, the recipients of the rebuke are the members of the churches who are in danger of being deceived by these deceivers.

The nature of the action Titus commanded is significant. The word "reprove" is the same rendered "convict" in verse 9, and should be so rendered here. Titus is to keep on convicting them, beating down the views of the false teachers and leading to a confession where there has been a yielding to the error. And he is to act "sharply." The word comes from a verb which means "to cut." "As a surgeon's knife cuts away the diseased and mortifying flesh, so must the words and discipline of Titus, the apostle's representative in Crete, sharply rebuke, and, if need be, punish the sinning members of the congregation" (Spence).

The contemplated result of this action is stated both positively and negatively. Positively, "that they may be sound in the faith." This is to be his continuing aim in dealing with them, that they may continue to enjoy spiritual health. That is what is at stake. "The faith," the Gospel truth which the enemies oppose, must be maintained. It is the sphere which constitutes the center and starting-point of the Christian life. If spiritual health is to continue "the faith" must be maintained. Personal faith becomes unhealthy when it continues to feed on unhealthy teaching.

The contemplated result is also negative. "Not giving heed to Jewish fables, and commandments of men who turn away from the truth." These Cretan deceivers, Paul points out, are spreading "fables," or myths. Their teachings are simply fictitious inventions, without factual basis. Believers are not to "give heed to" such things, must not willingly give their attention to them. "Men have not only no right to receive error, but they are under obligation to avoid it, to give no heed to it" (Harvey). These fables are but "the commandments of men." They lack divine authorization; hence are spurious. As seen from the following verse, these commandments relate to ritual observances and ceremonial rites. They are the commandments of men "who turn away from the truth." The force of the verb is, "they keep on turning themselves away from the truth." Such is their character. They offer positive proof of the close connection between doctrinal error and evil conduct.

c. The condemnation of the false teachers, vv. 15, 16. Paul closes the paragraph with certain great maxims which, when applied to the false teachers, demonstrate their condemnation. First he presents a test which operates in the realm of character, then in the realm of conduct.

1) The condemnation from the test of character, v. 15. "To the pure all things are pure." In this maxim the reference is not to moral purity but rather to ceremonial and ritual purity. (Cf. I Tim. 4:3-5; Rom. 14:14.) "All things" refers not to things morally wrong, but to all such outward things as meats and drinks to which the distinctions of pure and impure could be applied. These false teachers placed great emphasis upon such outward distinctions and rites connected therewith and the whole tendency of their teaching was to lay the stress upon the merely external. Those who kept their external regulations they considered pure; those who did not were condemned as being impure and unclean.

Paul teaches that the true criterion lies not in these external nonmoral things but in the nature of the inner life. Things in themselves have no moral character; they get their moral significance from the spirit of the user. The things of daily life are transformed by the spirit in which they are used. To the pure all things are pure for their use. "Inward purity leaves the impress of purity upon material surroundings and objects; these receive their character from the holy life spent among them" (Pope).

But the opposite is also true. "To them that are defiled and unbelieving nothing is pure." That they impute impurity to nonmoral things shows their inner character. They are in a state of being polluted and characterized as unbelievers.

"They have within a fountain of pollution which

spreads itself over and infects everything about them. Their food and drink, their possessions, their employments, their comforts, their actions—all are in the reckoning of God tainted with impurity, because they are putting away from them that which alone has for the soul regenerating and cleansing efficacy" (Fairbairn, quoted by Harvey).

"Both their mind and their conscience are defiled." Their whole inner being is polluted and perverted. Their rational nature and intellectual apprehension are perverted by their inner defilement, and their conscience has lost its sense of discrimination between what is innocent and what is sinful. By the test of their inner nature they stand condemned.

2) The condemnation from the test of conduct, v. 16. They also stand condemned when tested by the relationship between profession and conduct. "They profess that they know God." They openly place themselves within the ranks of Christians. Their public confession is that they are fully informed about God. "But by their works they deny him." By their conduct they practically deny all that which their lips affirm. They stand in a self-contradictory position. Paul, like John, knows that whenever there is a conflict between a man's talk and his walk, it is always his walk and not his talk that truly reveals what he is. By this test they are revealed as being "abominable, and disobedient, and unto every good work reprobate." In character they are "abominable," vile and detestable before God; in conduct they are "disobedient," refusing to submit to and follow the truth of God. Consequently they must be evaluated as being "reprobate." They have been tested for genuineness, like coins and metals, and have been proved to be spurious. They are only fit to be utterly rejected. In regard to every good work, all that is truly beneficial, they have shown themselves worthless.

II. CONCERNING THE NATURAL GROUPS IN THE CONGREGATIONS, 2:1-15

From the ghastly picture of the false teachers and the baneful results of their errors, the apostle turns to a consideration of the ethical obligations which the Gospel places upon believers. The entire paragraph stressed the fact that sound doctrine must find its fruitage in good deeds. The Gospel places this obligation upon every believer regardless of the station of life in which he may find himself. The Christian's duty and usefulness lie exactly in, not outside of, the circumstances under which his life is lived.

In this second division Paul passes from the subject of church organization and qualified leadership to a consideration of the duties of the various groups which compose the congregation. It may be divided into three sections. In verses 1-10 Paul sets forth the kind of life expected of each group in the congregation. Next he holds before us the grace of God as the motivating power of the Christian life (vv. 11-14). The division closes with a pointed restatement of the duty of Titus to maintain his ministerial authority (v. 15).

1. The Instructions to the Groups as to Character and Conduct, vv. 1-10

But speak thou the things which befit the sound doctrine: that aged men be temperate, grave, sober-minded, sound in faith, in love, in patience: that aged women likewise be reverent in demeanor, not slanderers nor enslaved to much wine, teachers of that which is good; that they may train the young women to love their husbands, to love their children, to be sober-minded, chaste, workers at home, kind, being in subjection to their own husbands, that the word of God be not blasphemed: the younger men likewise exhort to be sober-minded: in all things showing thyself an ensample of good works; in thy doctrine showing uncorruptness, gravity, sound speech, that cannot be condemned; that he that is of the contrary part may be ashamed, having no evil thing to say of us. Exhort servants to be in subjection to their own masters, and to be well-pleasing to them in all things; not gainsaying; not purloining, but showing all good fidelity; that they may adorn the doctrine of God our Saviour in all things.

We divide the paragraph into four parts. Titus is reminded of his duty properly to instruct the members in ethical conduct (v. 1); the desired character and conduct for the various age groups is set forth (vv. 2-6); parenthetically he stresses the importance of the personal example of Titus (vv. 7, 8); special instructions are added for the slaves (vv. 9, 10).

a. The duty of Titus properly to instruct the members, v. 1. "But speak thou the things which befit the sound doctrine." The "thou" is emphatic in the Greek and sets Titus in contrast to the false teachers. They were teaching "things which they ought not" (1:11). Their false doctrines were already producing their sure fruits in the form of a life utterly contrary to the true nature of the Gospel. Their myths and man-made prescriptions could only generate morbid sentiments about life and duty, since they lacked a valid basis. But the preaching of Titus is founded on the unshaken verities of the Christian Gospel. He must teach "sound doctrine" as actively as they teach error. The Gospel, as the vehicle of Christ's healing power over the soul of everyone that believeth, is not only healthful in its nature but bears healthfully on the conduct of men. Boldly and plainly he must continue to set forth the things which "befit" the Gospel. Believers must maintain a conduct becoming and appropriate to the healthful doctrine. It is the duty of every minister in all frankness and clarity to present to the people the becoming effect of the Gospel in the conduct of the believer.

b. The instructions relative to various age groups, vv.

2-6. He depicts the befitting things which Titus is to inculcate in the members. The instructions are grouped according to the age and sex of the members. He begins with the old as having most influence in their group relations.

1) The instructions concerning the older men, v. 2. "Aged men" has reference not to office, as some have thought, but to age, the old men of the congregation. They play a very important part in the life of the church. But the extent of their influence will depend wholly upon the sweetness and mellowness of their Christian character. Four characteristics are insisted upon. (1) "Temperate." The Greek word literally means "unmixed with wine, wineless," then of persons, "sober." The use of the term here doubtless includes this literal significance, but it has a wider connotation. They are to be sober and fully rational, in possession of the full use of all their faculties, in thought, word, and action. (2) "Grave." The word suggests that gravity and dignity of bearing which invites respect and reverence. (3) "Sober-minded." The word presents the concept of a well-balanced, properly regulated mind; a person discreet and prudent. The old men should be the balance wheels in the congregation, keeping its course steady. (4) "Sound in faith, in love, in patience." They are to be sound in health, without internal weakness, in regard to the trilogy of virtues—"faith, love, patience." The use of the articles in the original makes them prominent, "their faith, their love, their patience." They are recognized essentials of Christian character. They are to be strong and robust in their personal faith, tender and mellow, rather than bitter and vindictive, in their love, and characterized by patience. "Patience," or endurance here replaces "hope" in the trilogy. It pictures that brave patience with which the Christian endures the trials and tribulations of life without losing heart or courage. It is very needful in old age

with its increasing infirmities, disappointed aspirations, and growing loneliness. "It is the blessed office of the religion of Christ at such a time to lift the soul above querulousness and murmuring and despair, and inspire it with patient resignation, heavenly fortitude, and ever brightening hope; and it is where this effect is produced in the actual life, the Gospel shines forth in its highest glory before men" (Harvey).

2) The instructions concerning the elderly women, v. 3. As the old men, the "aged women likewise" must show Christian character traits. As fellow heirs of the grace of God they too have a grave responsibility. The first characteristic is general, "reverent in demeanor." The word "demeanor" denotes the entire external deportment as manifesting the inner life. The word "reverent" is a compound form, meaning "as is befitting or becoming sacred persons." "Priest-like" gives the thought. There is to be about their life that reverential spirit of consecration consistent with the fact of their spiritual priesthood. What a benediction and inspiration for service such a saintly grandmother can be in her family circle!

Three particulars, two negative, one positive, are added. "Not slanderers." The word, in the singular, is translated "devil" and means one speaking evil of or making accusations against others. As Spence observed, "Old age is at times intolerant, censorious, even bitter, forgetful especially of the days of youth; but Christ's aged saints must use their voice for better things than these." "Not enslaved to much wine." The tense (perfect) of the original denotes the state of being enslaved; it was a common vice among oriental women. "In the case of no sin is the bondage more conspicuous than in the case of drunkenness" (Bernard). Christianity must deliver from this bondage.

Positively, these older Christian women have something better to do. They are to be "teachers of that which is good." As seen from the next verse, they are the natural teachers in the home, and they are to teach that which is noble and attractive by precept and example.

3) The instructions concerning the young women, vv. 4, 5. Paul points out that he expects the old women, rather than Titus, to be the teachers of the young women; it is a domestic function. The word rendered "train" properly means "to make sober-minded." This is done by purposeful discipline and holding one to his duty. By thus training her daughters the Christian mother multiplies and perpetuates her usefulness in the homes of her children.

Seven characteristics are to be instilled. The first two form a pair: "to love their husbands, to love their children." Their first duty is to make home life attractive and beautiful by love of husband and children. "Love is the highest blessing in an earthly home, and of this the wife and mother is the natural center" (Harvey). Modern trends show how vitally necessary affectionate wives and mothers are today. The next pair relates to personal character: "sober-minded, chaste." They are to be balanced in act and judgment, discreet in all of their relations. They are to manifest purity in thought, word, and deed by a habitual self-restraint which gives no ground for evil reports. The third pair sets forth her position as queen in the home: "workers at home, kind." The rendering "keepers at home" in the King James Version is based on a slightly different reading. The reading of the American Standard Version is preferable and agrees better with the condemnation of idleness in I Timothy 5:13, 14. The home is pre-eminently the sphere of the woman's work. Christian women should be the best of housekeepers and models to others. And in her position as queen in the home she will be gentle and considerate as she dispenses all that is good and beneficial in this domain. The seventh item, "being in subjection to their own husbands," rules out any thought that the Gospel alters the established relation between husband and wife. The form might better be rendered, "submitting themselves to—" (middle rather than passive) to indicate that the Christian wife will voluntarily accept this divinely ordained relation to her husband. The requirement that she should "love her husband" does not eliminate this duty. Neither characteristic is of the right quality unless it includes the other.

Paul has more to say about these young women than about any of the other groups. The impact of their lives is of vital importance to the cause of Christianity. This Paul indicates by the added purpose clause, "that the word of God be not blasphemed." The connection of the clause is not to be confined to the last mentioned characteristic. It refers back to the entire preceding exhortation, including even the old women, since they are to produce such qualities in the young women. If the women of the church fail to manifest such character Paul fears lest the whole Gospel be vilified. The world still judges the churches largely by the character of its women. Paul is anxious to avoid any suspicion that the spiritual freedom gained by the women in Christianity makes less dutiful wives and mothers. The elevating and refining impact of Christianity upon womanhood is one of the significant social contributions of Christianity.

4) The instructions concerning the younger men, v. 6. "The younger men" includes all those not yet classified as "old men." The duty of exhorting these younger men is assigned directly to Titus. His method of influencing them will be through the use of brotherly exhortation. He will not use a domineering, high-handed attitude but will resort to kindly appeal. To such an approach the heart of the younger men will respond.

Only one demand is made upon the younger men. They are "to be sober-minded." This characteristic receives special emphasis because of its repetition (cf. 1:8; 2:2, 4,

5). They are to cultivate balance and self-restraint; their faculties, appetites, and passions must be kept under the control of a sound judgment and an enlightened conscience. It is a comprehensive demand that covers all of their lives.

c. The personal example of Titus, vv. 7, 8. According to age, Titus himself would belong to the younger men. His duty to exhort the younger men leads Paul to an exhortation to Titus himself to be what he wishes them to be. It is parenthetic in nature and stands between the two sets of instructions to the members.

Titus is continually to set a personal example before the people. He is himself (emphatic by position) to be the example: "showing thyself an ensample." It is not enough for the minister merely to set the ideal before the people; he must embody it in his own life. A congregation has a right to expect its minister to exemplify in daily life that which he urges upon them. He must set the pattern for them. An acted sermon is more readily understood than an elaborate pulpit discourse. It is to be feared that not a few ministers today fall under the condemnation which Jesus pronounced upon the Pharisees, "they say, and do not" (Matt. 23:3).

The example is to be comprehensive, "in all things," all that Titus urges upon them. It relates to both his conduct and his teaching. In his conduct he is to be "an ensample of good works." In all activity that is attractive and excellent he is to set the example. As the apostolic representative, his teaching likewise must be exemplary in manner and content. "In thy doctrine showing uncorruptness, gravity." These two attributes have reference to the attitude and manner of the teacher, rather than to the content of the teaching. To make the first refer to the substance of the teaching, as some do, is to anticipate what is said in the next verse. His attitude in all his teaching is not to be self-seeking; he must preach without fear or favor. In manner he is to show "gravity," to manifest a dignity appropriate to the nature of the sacred message. The added word "sincerity," found in the King James Version, must be omitted for lack of manuscript authority. The substance of his teaching is described as "sound speech, that cannot be condemned." It is characterized as "healthy" (adjective) teaching, standing in contrast to the unhealthy teaching of the false teachers. Robust spiritual health is dependent upon healthful teaching. It is further described as teaching "that cannot be condemned." It reminds us that the Christian teacher must use great care not to say anything rash or reprehensible, thereby offering occasion for criticism and condemnation. But it implies that even "sound teaching" may be criticized and spoken against, but after being given a fair trial and found not wanting, it will be acquitted. What a searching test this puts upon the teaching ministry! Well may the minister resolve with the psalmist: "I will keep my mouth with a bridle, while the wicked is before me" (Ps. 39:1).

The contemplated result of the example of Titus is "that he that is of the contrary part may be ashamed, having no evil thing to say of us." The use of the singular "he" makes the opponent the representative of the class. By his exemplary life and faultless teaching this opponent will effectively be put to shame when it is seen that he has no case. The purity of life enforcing the teaching will leave him no basis to speak any evil "of us." The reading "us" instead of "you" has the weight of manuscript authority. By its use Paul identifies himself with Titus and all Christian workers. Any failure on the part of Titus would reflect directly on Paul. Whenever a minister fails, his failure casts reproach upon the entire brotherhood of believers. May God give us grace to work circumspectly so as not to bring reproach upon His church and our Lord Jesus Christ!

d. The exhortation to the slaves, vv. 9, 10. Paul has been giving instructions for the old men and women and the young women and men. But there was one group which overlapped all of these groups. They were the slaves. The former grouping was based on age and sex, this is based on social status. Slaves formed a considerable element in all the apostolic churches. The very difficulty of their position made it necessary that special instructions be given to them. The dignity and spiritual freedom which they were experiencing in the assembly must not blind them to the fact that Christianity did not relieve them of their obligations arising out of their status in society. Paul holds before them the attitude which is to govern their relations to their masters (v.9), points out their conduct as Christians (vv.9c, 10a), and enforces it by setting forth the Christian motive for such conduct (v.10b).

1) The attitude enjoined upon the slaves, v. 9. "Exhort servants to be in subjection to their own masters." The word "master," from which we get our English word despot, denotes one who has absolute ownership and uncontrolled power over his slave. The slave was entirely at the mercy of his master. They are urged voluntarily to be subject to their masters as a matter of principle. But their subjection is not to be yielded in a reluctant, sulking, and bitter manner. They are actively to seek to be "well-pleasing to them in all things." This is the distinctive element which Christianity adds to the attitude of the slave. Alford says that this is a servant's term, like our English "to give satisfaction."

2) The conduct of the slaves, vv. 9c, 10a. The preceding points have already indicated the general nature of their conduct. Paul now adds two negative and one positive particular to describe their conduct. First negatively, "not gainsaying." The word includes all forms of opposition, whether by word or action, "Not purloining." The refer-

ence is to that form of theft which retains for oneself part of something which has been entrusted to one's care. The term includes more than just petty thievery. As Humphreys points out: "Almost all trades, arts, and professions were at this time in the hands of slaves; and so all tricks of trade, all mercantile or professional embezzlement and dishonesty, are covered by the word."

Positively, they are to be "showing all good fidelity." They are to show themselves faithful and trustworthy in every matter entrusted to them. Their fidelity is to be true and genuine, as opposed to mere assumed surface obedience and service. But Paul places a limit on that fidelity by saying "all good fidelity." It is to be shown in everything that is good and beneficial. As Hervey remarks: "The duty of fidelity does not extend to crime or wrong-doing."

3) The motive for such conduct, v. 10b. Paul enforces this demand for becoming conduct with a profound spiritual motive. "That they may adorn the doctrine of God our Saviour in all things." In verse 5 the motive advanced was negative; here it is positive. The two are complementary. The desire of the slave will be to make attractive "the doctrine of God our Saviour." That doctrine has brought to him the knowledge and assurance of eternal life and it is his Christian purpose to make it known to others. But his pagan master would show but little interest in it as an abstract theory. To make it appealing and attractive to his master he would have to exemplify it in his service. Thus the lowly slave had the opportunity to "ornament" the doctrine of God. "It was reserved for the gospel to teach that in the lowly duties of a slave as such, it was possible to bring luster to the sublimest truth of revelation, the truth that God is Himself our Saviour" (Horton).

2. The Grace of God as the Motive Power for the Christian Life, vv. 11, 14

> For the grace of God hath appeared, bringing salvation to all men, instructing us, to the intent that, denying ungodliness and worldly lusts, we should live soberly and righteously and godly in this present world; looking for the blessed hope and appearing of the glory of the great God and our Saviour Jesus Christ; who gave himself for us, that he might redeem us from all iniquity, and purify unto himself a people for his own possession, zealous of good works.

The opening "for" intimately relates this weighty sentence with the practical duties which have been stressed. In typical Pauline fashion the prosaic duties of everyday life are undergirded and enforced by this masterful summation of Christian doctrine and practice. Christian conduct must be grounded in and motivated by the power of revealed truth. The statement is an unfolding of the meaning of the phrase "God our Saviour" (v. 10). Humphreys calls this passage "the first of the two Evangelical outbursts of that 'spring of living water' in St. Paul's own heart which kept his life and teaching always green and fresh." And who but Paul could have written such a sentence?

a. The manifestation of the grace of God, v. 11. "For the grace of God hath appeared." Turning to the past, Paul asserts the historical manifestation of the grace of God. It is the source of our salvation. "The grace of God" is His unmerited favor toward men expressing itself in active love in procuring our redemption in Christ Jesus. "Hath appeared" (aorist tense) marks the reality as a fact in history. God's manifestation of His grace began with Christ's Incarnation but includes His life, death, and resurrection. In view of the training ministry ascribed to this grace in the next verse, may it not be that Paul also includes in the manifestation the founding of the church at Pentecost and the subsequent ministry of the apostles?

This grace is described as "bringing salvation." The

original is an adjective (sōtērios) meaning "saving, bringing salvation." It describes the effect of this grace as being beneficent and redemptive. It brings salvation "to all men." It is a question whether "to all men" is to be associated with "hath appeared," as in the King James Version, or with "bringing salvation." This latter connection is followed in the text of the American Standard Version, with the alternative in the footnote. The former reading cannot mean that it has actually appeared to all men. After more than nineteen centuries there are still multitudes to whom the fact of this manifestation of grace in the First Advent has not yet been made known. The dative may be rendered "for all men," thus indicating the intended scope of the grace that was manifested. The context, however, favors the other connection. Thus viewed, it is descriptive of the universality of the salvation provided in Christ; it is adapted to and freely available to all men. No nation, tongue, class, or group was excluded. The atonement rendered all men saveable. This does not mean that all men will be saved, since its power actually to save is dependent upon personal faith.

b. The instruction of the grace of God, v. 12. The recipients of this instruction Paul designates as "us," those who have personally accepted the grace of God for salvation. The participle translated "instructing" indicates the nature of the instruction. The verb *paideuō*, from which we get our English word "pedagogue," has no exact equivalent in the English. It does at times have the force of "instruct," as in Acts 7:22; 22:3, etc., but quite literally it means "to train a child, to bring up a child." In this child-training process instruction does have a prominent part. But every parent knows that the process at times also requires rebuke and chastisement. Notwithstanding the assertions of some learned modern psychologists, the timely use of some physical persuasion on the posterior end is truly beneficial for the development of the child.

So grace takes the believer into its school and carries on the process of training us. Knowledge of things spiritual is given, but when that is not enough then rebuke, conviction, and chastening are administered. The final aim is not creed but character. Accordingly we are told: "Whom the Lord loveth he chasteneth, and scourgeth every son whom he receiveth" (Heb. 12:6). The present tense indicates that this is a continuing process. No one ever graduates from the school of God's grace in this life.

The aim of this educative process is stated both negatively and positively. "To the intent that, denying ungodliness and worldly lusts, we should live soberly and righteously and godly." The Gospel offers not merely an escape from the punishment of sin but aims to effect a transformation in the character and conduct of the saved. Jesus does not save His people in their sin but from their sin. Due to man's sinful past, there must first be a negative work, a clearing away of the rubbish before there can be constructive building. Everything offensive to God and contrary to grace must be renounced. "Denying ungodliness and worldly lusts." The force of the tense (aorist) may well be rendered, "having denied or renounced," pointing to a definite act of renunciation. Such an act of renunciation, standing at the beginning of a life of experiential victory, must be carried into effect by daily self-denial.

The sins to be renounced have a Godward and a worldward reference. "Ungodliness" denotes want of reverence toward God, hence is suggestive of the whole inner and outer life of the one who lives without God and in opposition to His law. An ungodly man is not necessarily a wicked, outbroken sinner but one who, however moral his conduct, has no place for God in his life. "Worldly lusts" are those desires which are limited to and characterized by this world as estranged from God. Since he has no place for God in his life, the desires and yearnings of the unsaved man are occupied with the things of this passing world. These things the grace of God trains the believer to renounce.

But the Christian must have more than just the negative virtues which result from giving up sin. We must also cultivate the positive virtues. "We should live soberly and righteously and godly." In the original these three adverbs stand before the verb and are emphatic. While no sharp division between them should be pressed, they may well be regarded as indicating respectively our duty to ourself, to our neighbor, and to God. (1) "Soberly." For the fifth and last time sobriety is mentioned (see 1:8; 2:2, 4, 5, 6). But now it is not applied to a specific group but is given as the characteristic of every true believer. (2) "Righteously." In relation to our fellow men God's grace requires of us a life of truth and strict justice in all our dealings. (3) "Godly." The old attitude of indifference to God has been replaced by an attitude of supreme devotion to Him. Once we had no place for God in our lives; now we are ever conscious of living in His presence and desire to fulfill all our duties toward Him. The world instinctively recognizes the contradiction in Christian profession when these characteristics are lacking.

"This present world," or "the present course of things " is the sphere where such a life is to be lived. It relates to the present, not to the life beyond. It is expected of us now. If Paul thought it possible for the believers amid the degraded environment on Crete, surely we cannot excuse ourselves by blaming our failure on our adverse circumstances. Those who receive the instruction of the grace of God are enabled to live thus.

c. The expectation of Christ's return, v. 13. The present trying circumstances naturally turn our thought to the future. "Looking for the blessed hope." The agreement of the participle with the personal pronoun "we" in the verse above reminds us that those who possess this

hope are the ones who are experiencing the present discipline of the grace of God. If we do not cherish this
"blessed hope" is it because we are "tardy" scholars in the
school of grace? The tense indicates that this is the constant attitude of the believer. The word implies an attitude of eager expectancy, a readiness to welcome the one
being awaited.

The object of our expectation is "the blessed hope and
appearing of the glory." Paul is not setting forth the two
phases of the second advent, the rapture ("the blessed
hope") and the revelation ("the glorious appearing") as
the King James rendering might suggest. Both hope and
appearing are under the government of one article, thus
uniting them. He is thinking of our Lord's return in
glory, but considered from two different viewpoints. For
the believer it is "the blessed hope." Hope is not used
here subjectively of our attitude of hope but objectively
of the thing hoped for. The consummation of all our
blessings are vitally related to the return of our Lord.
For our Lord Himself it is the "appearing in glory" (not
"the glorious appearing" as the King James has it). For
Him it will mean the manifestation of His glory, now
unrecognized and disregarded by the world. In verse 11
we had the past epiphany in grace; here the future epiphany in glory.

When He thus returns "in glory," whose glory is it?
"The glory of the great God and our Saviour Jesus
Christ." Is Paul referring to two Persons or to only
Christ Himself? Grammatically both views are possible,
and views have been sharply divided on the question. We
regard the whole expression as designating Christ for
the following reasons: (1) The government of both nouns
in the Greek under one article naturally suggests this
view, although this is not decisive. (2) The relative clause
"who gave himself" (v. 14) plainly refers to Christ only,
but the construction naturally leads us to take the whole

preceding expression as its antecedent. (3) The word "appearing" (*epiphaneia*) is habitually used by Paul of Christ's First or Second Advent, but not of the Father. (4) The application of the adjective "great" is rather pointless if applied to the Father, but it is highly significant if applied to Christ in a context which emphasizes the greatness of the fact that He gave Himself. (5) The designation of Christ as God is in harmony with other Scripture (John 20:28; Rom. 9:5; Heb. 1:8; II Peter 1:1). (6) The Greek and Latin Fathers, with few exceptions, so understood it. (But the early versions generally adopted the other rendering.)

Accepting this view, we have here a definite ascription of deity to Jesus Christ—"the great God," an expression unique in the New Testament. Even those expositors who adhere to the other view admit that the passage is a clear testimony to the deity of Christ. Those who distinguish two Persons hold that Paul means that Christ appears in the glory of the Father (Matt. 16:27; Mark 8:38), and at the same time in His own glory (Matt. 25:31). On this view, by asserting His equality in glory with the Father, which would be blasphemy if predicated of any mere man, His deity is equally indicated.

At His First Advent the claims of Christ to deity were scornfully rejected by His enemies and made the basis for His condemnation. But His claims will be vindicated when He returns in open glory with His saints to earth. In that day our Lord, whom not having seen we love (I Peter 1:8), will be manifested as "our Saviour," consummating our salvation in eternal glory.

d. The purpose of Christ's redemption, v. 14. With this summary statement of redemption Paul returns to the present to stress again the truth of Christian sanctification. The redemption was wrought through our Saviour's self-sacrifice. "Who gave himself for us." It was a definite, voluntary act on His part. It was an exhaustive act, "Himself," His whole unique personality. It was substitutionary, "for us." Since He gave Himself "to redeem" us, it is impossible to exclude the idea of substitution from the verse. He freed us by giving "himself a ransom for all" (I Tim. 2:6; Matt. 20:28; Mark 10:45).

The purpose in the redemption is viewed both negatively and positively. Negatively, "that he might redeem us from all iniquity." Our condition of bondage in iniquity had to be undone. The redemption is here viewed as rescuing us from the power rather than the guilt of sin. The preposition used (*apo*) denotes the completeness of the deliverance. The word "iniquity" is literally "lawlessness," the word used in I John 3:4. It speaks of that contempt for and violation of God's law which characterizes the unbeliever as a rebel against God.

The redemptive purpose was also positive, "and purify unto himself a people for his own possession." The figure of purification presupposes a previous defilement by sin. Sin not only makes us guilty but also dirty. Those who have been cleansed are now "a people for his own possession." As redeemed and purified we belong to Christ as His special possession or treasure. The rendering "a peculiar people" in the King James Version means that which is one's private possession. It does not mean that believers are to be strange, odd, and ridiculous in their clothing, manners, and customs. But by character and conduct we are to reveal the fact that we are not our own but belong wholly to Him. As such we must be characterized as being "zealous of good works." "Every Christian should not merely be good, but be full of burning zeal in doing good" (Brown). That believer who eagerly awaits the return of his Lord will endeavor to do his utmost by good works to further the cause of his Lord.

3. The Restatement of the Duty of Titus, v. 15

These things speak and exhort and reprove with all authority. Let no man despise thee.

Paul concludes the chapter with a restatement of the
duty of Titus, urging him actively to inculcate the moral
precepts set forth in the first section of the chapter and to
maintain his ministerial authority.

"Speak and exhort and reprove." The present impera-
tives imply that Titus is busy doing these things and that
he is to continue thus. The three words set forth the function of the minister. (1) "Speak." He is clearly to set forth
"these things," the presentation of the will of God. He
must speak the whole truth and it alone, no unfounded
human speculation. (2) "Exhort." He must apply the
truth to local circumstances and urge the people to follow
it. (3) "Reprove," or better "convict." He must rebuke
those who neglect their duty and bring conviction upon
them for it. And this he must do "with all authority." As
God's will is made known, God's people have no choice as
to whether they want to obey or not. The message must be
delivered to them as God's command. Thus his is the
authority of the truth itself. The ministry of Titus rests
not merely on the authority he has received from Paul
but on the truth itself. "The phrase, rightly understood,
does not raise the minister above the truth, but the truth
above the minister" (Horton). It is not presumption, but
rather the plain duty of the minister to speak the Gospel
with all authority.

Mindful of the difficult task of Titus, Paul adds the
warning, "Let no man despise thee." It is not a warning
that Titus is not to allow anyone to "look down on him"
(*kataphroneō*). The word here used (*periphroneō*) literally means "to think around," hence, "to disregard by setting oneself in thought beyond." It is the picture of a
man attempting to rationalize himself into a position
where he can evade these responsibilities and so continue

on in his old sins. Such a rejection of his authority Titus must not allow.

III. CONCERNING BELIEVERS AMONG MEN GENERALLY, 3:1-11

In this division Paul widens the scope of his consideration to deal with the conduct of believers in relation to government and society generally. The preceding instructions, except for the brief reference to the relation of the slave to his master, have viewed the believer in his relations to follow Christians. He now shows that the obligations of the Gospel are operative also in the believer's relations to government and pagan society.

This paragraph may be divided into three sections. He sets forth the believer's obligations to government and society (vv. 1, 2), advances three considerations as undergirding these obligations (vv. 3-8a), and concludes the body of the Epistle with a summary statement of the proper reaction to spiritual truth and error (vv. 8b-11).

Put them in mind to be in subjection to rulers, to authorities, to be obedient, to be ready unto every good work, to speak evil of no man, not to be contentious, to be gentle, showing all meekness toward all men. For we also once were foolish, disobedient, deceived, serving divers lusts and pleasures, living in malice and envy, hateful and hating one another. But when the kindness of God our Saviour, and his love toward man, appeared, not by works done in righteousness, which we did ourselves, but according to his mercy he saved us, through the washing of regeneration and renewing of the Holy Spirit, which he poured out upon us richly, through Jesus Christ our Saviour; that, being justified by his grace, we might be made heirs according to the hope of eternal life. Faithful is the saying, and concerning these things I desire that thou affirm confidently, to the end that they who have believed God may be careful to maintain good works. These things are good and profitable

unto men: but shun foolish questionings, and genealogies, and strifes, and fightings about the law; for they
are unprofitable and vain. A factious man after a first
and second admonition refuse; knowing that such a one
is perverted, and sinneth, being self-condemned.

1. The Obligations of Believers as Citizens, vv. 1, 2

Christianity makes better citizens of people. It does not
relieve them of their civic duties but rather enforces them.
As citizens of the State they have obligations to the gov-
ernment (v. 1), as well as to the citizens of the State (v. 2).
Titus is urged to impress this matter upon the Cretan
Christians.

a. The obligations in relation to government, v. 1. "Put
them in mind to be in subjection to rulers." "Them"
means all the Christians on Crete. The exhortation is not
due solely to the turbulent character of the Cretans. Similar precepts are also given in other epistles (Rom. 13:1-7;
I Peter 3:8-17). All Christians need this exhortation, but
the well-known turbulence of the Cretans and the large
number of Jews on the island made the matter timely.
Hence Titus must "put them in mind" about these duties.
The present imperative implies that he must continue doing so. He is to "cause them to remember," implying that
they already knew about the duties but needed to have
them impressed afresh on their consciousness.

The Christian's duty is "to be in subjection to rulers, to
authorities." The present middle infinitive means that
they are voluntarily to be subjecting themselves to government, "to rulers, to authorities." The two abstract
terms designate government as such without indicating
any particular form or person. As the institution of God,
Christians must be subject to government. A Christian
cannot be an anarchist.

The implications of this subjection to government are
further indicated by the words "to obey, to be ready unto
every good work." "To obey" has the thought of obedi-

ence to a superior and seems to denote obedience to particular commands of government, such as payment of taxes, dues, etc. The only limitation upon this obedience is when it involves disobedience to God, but even then the apostles, while firmly refusing to obey, submitted to the penalty (Acts 4:19, 20; 5:29, 40, 41). "To be ready unto every good work," from the connection, seems to have reference to work started by government, and includes civic and municipal duties. The attitude of the Christian toward government should be positive. As a citizen he must co-operate with and seek to further all that is beneficial to the State and to society. The word "good" again points to a limitation on the duty; that which is not good he will refuse to promote.

b. The obligation in relation to citizens generally, v. 2. The naming of a new object "no man" (emphatic by position) shows that from this point on he is no longer speaking of specific duties to government, but of duties to citizens generally. These duties are indicated both negatively and positively. On the negative side, two common snares are prohibited. "To speak evil of no man." That does not mean that they are never to talk of and expose the evils of men, for Jesus Himself did so very forcefully. It means that they are not to malign, slander, or speak injuriously of others. Prevailing practices made this a constant snare to believers, for as Brown remarks, "verbal abuse is practiced as a fine art in the East." Further, believers are "not to be contentious." They must not pick up an occasion for a fight, must abstain from being quarrelsome. "People who are ever fighting are wretched citizens and neighbors" (Lenski).

They are rather to manifest positive virtues, "to be gentle, showing all meekness toward all men." The word "gentle" is the very opposite of "contentious." Instead of being aggressive and pugnacious, they are to be actively considerate and forbearing, not insisting on their own rights. They are to show a "sweet reasonableness," to borrow the phrase of Matthew Arnold, and be indulgent toward the infirmities of the unsaved. "Meekness" is that unassuming inner spirit of mildness and gentleness which is the opposite of haughtiness, harshness, and self-assertiveness. Such a spirit, as the form of the participle implies *(endeiknumenous)*, they are to continue showing forth as something that is their own, something within them, not something that is merely put on from the outside. And this grace of "meekness" is to be exhibited not only in their dealings with fellow believers but "toward all men," as the appropriate mark of the followers of Him who Himself was "meek" (Matt. 11:29).

2. The Motives for Such a Godly Life, vv. 3-8a

In a grand passage the apostle once again advances weighty truths to undergird and motivate the exhortations just given. In this masterly outline of evangelical teaching, he stresses not the disciplining effect of grace on the believer, as in chapter 2, but rather emphasizes the transforming effect of God's kindness in the life of Christians. In typical Pauline fashion he sets forth the contrast between what we once were (v. 3) and what grace has done for us (vv. 4-7). These profound doctrinal realities demand from us a life consistent therewith (v. 8a).

a. The motive from our past life, v. 3. When we recall what "we too once were" ("we" emphatic by position), we have reason to be gentle and meek toward the unsaved. We must not forget from what we have been saved. By his use of "we" Paul includes himself in this description of our past life. He starts with the inner condition and then shows its outward expression. The word "foolish," without understanding, lacking in spiritual discernment, gives a general description of the inner spiritual condition. Because of sin, the mind of fallen man has become wholly perverted (Rom. 1:28). The result is that sinners are "disobedient, deceived." The first term depicts their attitude as being impersuasible and uncompliant toward God and His law, while the second pictures them as being led astray and made to wander from the path of truth, deceived by false religious systems and led on by their own lusts. The resultant life is described, first, as to its governing desires, and then as to its loveless reactions. "Serving divers lusts and pleasures." Impelled by their motley lusts and pleasures, allowing them to dictate their will, they have become the slaves of them. As Brown remarks: "With a sort of grim humor S. Paul here flashes a sudden light on what is called a 'life of pleasure,' and shows what a slavery it really is." They are living, spending their lives, "in malice and envy," words descriptive of their habitual disposition. "Malice" is that evil attitude of mind which manifests itself in ill-will and desire to injure, while "envy" begrudges others their good fortune. The fearful outcome was the lovelessness of pagan society: "hateful, hating one another." Their detestable character and malignant disposition aroused mutual repulsion and antagonism, thus promoting the dissolution of the bonds of human society.

In Romans 1 Paul has given an expansion of this brief picture. Not all the unsaved manifest these characteristics to the same extent but it is a picture of what depraved human nature naturally leads to. It is a depression picture. "Sin blunts the mind (foolish), perverts the heart and will (disobedient, going astray), stimulates carnal desires (lusts, pleasures), and encourages the growth of all forms of selfish feeling (malice, envy, hate)" (Lilley).

b. The motive from our present salvation, vv. 4-7. What we have become, in contrast to what we once were, furnishes a powerful motive for Christian living. What we are is no ground for self-exaltation, for the change is due entirely to God's salvation freely bestowed on us. This salvation he describes as to its source (v. 4), basis (v. 5a), means (vv. 5b, 6), and result (v. 7). We have here a passage of great theological importance, but it was conceived not for dogmatic reasons but for the enforcement of ethical precepts.

1) The source of the salvation, v. 4. Our salvation had its historical starting-point in "the kindness of God our Saviour, and his love toward man." Here we have two aspects of the grace mentioned in 2:11. The use of two articles in the original makes them distinct but they are so allied that the verb is in the singular. "The kindness of God" is His graciousness, His goodness which is ever ready to bestow blessing and forgiveness. His "love-toward-man" (our English word "philanthropy") is expressive of the fact of His feeling of pity toward man and that it extends to all men. The divine attitude thus stands in sharp contrast to the human disposition pictured in verse 3. Although God hates the sinner's sin, He loves the sinner and yearns to save him. God was the first great Philanthropist. True human philanthropy must be rooted in the divine love. "The goodness and love of God to man, on which our salvation is based, should lead us to show benevolence and gentleness to all men" (Huther).

The verb "hath appeared," also used in 2:11, implies that these qualities of God were always there but received a clear manifestation in the coming of Christ and the consequent proclamation of the Gospel. Glimpses of these characteristics had been given in the Old Testament, but it was especially in the proclamation of the Gospel that there was announced to the world this benignity of "God our Saviour." He now stands revealed in His character as Saviour. The "our" is highly confessional and appropriate for those in whom this salvation is being realized.

2) The basis of the salvation, v. 5a. "He saved us" states the saving act as a past fact; "us" denotes all those who have accepted Christ as Saviour. Although the salvation is still incomplete and awaits its consummation at the return of our Saviour, it is the present possession of all those who by faith have been united to Christ.

In typical Pauline fashion, the basis for this salvation is stated both negatively and positively. Negatively, we were saved "not by works done in righteousness, which we did ourselves." The "we" is emphatic; we did no works which merited or called forth God's salvation. Works wrought in the sphere of righteousness and acceptable to God, we did not do, nor were we able to do. Nothing on our part merited our salvation. Therefore, "according to his mercy he saved us." The positive ground of our salvation lies in God. The position of "his" makes it emphatic and marks the contrast with "we" in the preceding clause. The "mercy" of God, His self-moved, spontaneous compassion for sinful man, originated and wrought our salvation. No mention is here made of the human condition of faith because Paul is stressing the thought of God's interposition to save fallen man.

3) The means of the salvation, vv. 5b, 6. With the words "through the washing of regeneration and renewing of the Holy Spirit," Paul indicates the means whereby this salvation was effected in us. It was through the Spirit's regeneration and sanctification of the soul.

The word translated "washing" (*loutron*), which occurs only here and in Ephesians 5:26 in the New Testament, means either the place or water in which a bath is taken, or the act of bathing or washing. Both renderings are advocated here. "Washing" is preferred by our versions and has the support of classical usage. What is meant by "the washing of regeneration"? Answers differ.

One view refers it to the regenerating work by the Word of God. In Ephesians 5:26 Paul speaks of the cleansing of the church "by the washing of water with the word." The cleansing is effected through the application of the Word of God to heart and conscience. The Word is elsewhere pointed out as the instrument or means of regeneration (I Peter 1:23; James 1:18). As the revelation of the Word is applied to the heart, regeneration is wrought by the Spirit. It is the initial experience of salvation wrought within the believer. Baptism is the consequent testimony of the washing that has taken place.

If however, with the majority of commentators, we accept the washing as a reference to baptism, then baptism must be interpreted as the outward sign of the inner experience. In the New Testament baptism is the outward symbol of the inner spiritual reality and the two are never separated. Apart from the inner reality the outward symbol has no value. The rite of baptism does not produce the regeneration, but the Biblical writers at times use the symbol for the reality. They did not conceive of the symbol without the reality. No outward rite effects the spiritual change, a truth Paul clearly asserts in connection with circumcision (Rom. 2:25-29). But the New Testament clearly considers Christian baptism as the normal expression and accompaniment of faith. Paul assumes that the baptism of the believers was the occasion at which their faith in Christ had been openly confessed before men and had been confirmed by their inner consciousness of the experience of regeneration.

The word "regeneration," expressive of a new state of things, occurs only in Matthew 19:28 and here. Here it refers to the rebirth of the soul. In the words of Jesus in Matthew it has reference to the rebirth of external nature, creation, at the revelation of Christ in glory.

Grammatically, two constructions are possible of the words "the washing of regeneration and renewing of the Holy Spirit." One view regards both "regeneration" and "renewing" as dependent upon the word "washing." (See the text of the American Standard Version.) On this view the regeneration is further described as the renewing of the Holy Spirit, both pointing to the same divine act. The other construction holds that the preposition "through" governs both the washing of regeneration and the renewing of the Holy Spirit. This gives us two facts instead of just one. The renewing work of the Spirit, begun at regeneration, is then viewed as continuing in the life of the believer. We prefer this view. It is the reading given in the margin and is implied by the comma in the King James. In Ephesians 5:26 the mention of the cleansing of the church is supplemented by the thought of the sanctification of the church till there shall be no spot or blemish. In Romans 12:2 this renewal is presented as a continuing experience. It is the development and extension of the regeneration initiating the new life. It is the continuing work of the Spirit.

Verse 6 shows that God in the gift of the Spirit has made ample provision for the carrying out of this renewal. "Which [Spirit] He poured out upon us rightly." A faulty and inadequate experience of this renewal is always due to some human impediment. The tense of the verb "poured" (aorist) probably refers to Pentecost, when dispensationally the Holy Spirit was poured out upon the church. In the experience of each individual believer it points to the time of our new birth. "Through Jesus Christ our Saviour" gives the medium through which the Spirit's presence is secured to us. It speaks of the Incarnation as the condition essential to and preparatory for the coming of the Spirit. The application of the term "Saviour" to both the Father (v. 4) and the Son (v. 6) offers eloquent testimony to Paul's conviction concerning the deity of Christ. The confessional "our" points out once more the personal appropriation of Him as Saviour on our part.

Notice the reference to the Trinity. All three Persons of the Trinity are present in and co-operative in the work of grace, each having His special function in the salvation of our soul.

4) The results of the salvation, v. 7. Two results are indicated, both relating to the matter of our relation to God. The first is justification. "Being justified by his

grace." Sin disrupted our relation to God and estranged us from Him. But when we received Christ as our Saviour we were justified, declared righteous, given the standing as just and brought into His favor. Justification is an act of God's grace, originating in His free, unmerited favor. It is bestowed upon us in virtue of our union with Christ by faith. Justification relates to the matter of our standing before God, but it is never divorced from an actual change in the one declared righteous.

A further result is that we have been made heirs. This is not merely a future hope, but a present reality. The aim, "that we might be made heirs," has been achieved. As Huther says: "The apostle is speaking not of the future, but of the present condition of believers. They *are* heirs of eternal life; but they are so in hope, not yet in actual possession." The experiential realization of the inheritance awaits the day of our Lord's return. Our being heirs is in full accord with our "hope of eternal life." Eternal life is ours now but its consummation likewise awaits the time when Christ shall come for His church.

c. The motivation from the connection between doctrine and conduct, v. 8a. Paul proceeds to draw a lesson from this lofty doctrinal passage by pointing out the relation between doctrine and conduct. He evaluates these truths as reliable and fully trustworthy. With his utterance, "Faithful is the saying," he expresses his complete confidence in the sublime truths stated in verses 4-7. Therefore he urges that Titus in his teaching shall "affirm confidently" these truths. Such insistent proclamation has a definite purpose: "to the end that they who have believed God may be careful to maintain good works." Right beliefs must exhibit their fruits in life. Paul was confident that good works were the certain result of a theology which gave prominence to the free and unmerited grace of God to the sinner. It is the logical result of a true apprehension of the grace of God. This fact must be pressed upon those "who have believed God," whose faith, characterized as an abiding state, has brought them into personal relations with God Himself. They must give serious thought to this obligation "to maintain good works." It must be their care to "excel in good works," to be pre-eminent in the practice of them.

3. The Reaction to Spiritual Truth and Error, vv. 8b-11

Paul concludes the body of the Epistle by adding a note about the proper reaction to truth and error. The last part of verse 8 indicates the Christian evaluation of the truths advanced in this letter, while the next three verses set forth the necessary reaction to error.

a. The evaluation of "these things," v. 8b. With "these things" Paul summarizes the truths and duties laid down in the body of the letter. "These things are good and profitable unto men." They are excellent in themselves as spiritual verities and as such are profitable, valuable for beneficent and holy living. Titus and the Christians to whom they are given will recognize them as such. If such is their character they will also prove to be spiritually profitable to other people as well.

b. The attitude of Titus to spiritual error, vv. 9-11. But Titus will come into touch with things not of this character. He must make a negative reaction to false teaching (v. 9), as well as the factious individual (vv. 10, 11).

1) His attitude toward false teaching, v. 9. The reaction to take toward false teaching is indicated in the word "shun." Quite literally it means "to turn oneself about" for the purpose of avoiding something, thus "to avoid, shun." The tense points to a continuing attitude. The things to be shunned are "foolish questionings, and genealogies, and strifes, and fightings about the law." The words mark the content and spirit of the heretical Jewish teachings rampant on Crete. They were concerned with silly questions, the filling up of the genealogies of the

Old Testament, and the spinning of stories about these fictitious people. Attending to such teaching simply produced controversy and incessant strife. The reason for shunning them is because "they are unprofitable and vain." They are useless and morally fruitless, hence unworthy of time and serious consideration.

2) His attitude toward a factious person, vv. 10, 11. The individual under consideration is characterized as "a factious man." The term (*hairetikos*) occurs only here in the New Testament and means a person who is quarrelsome and stirs up factions through erroneous opinions, a man who is determined to go his own way and so forms parties and factions. His self-chosen opinions are those described in verse 9.

Such a man Titus is to deal with, giving him "a first and second admonition." He is to reprimand him once and again, administering a word of remonstrance, rebuke, and censure, with a view to reclaiming him. If this fails, he is to "refuse" him, have nothing to do with him, refuse to be bothered with him. All further attention is to be withdrawn from him, leaving him to himself. "Factious men and foolish errors are sometimes pushed into prominence by being controverted; whereas, if they were shunned, thoroughly let alone, they would of themselves come to nought. A very different rule of action is given in cases where the error is, not as in this case, foolish but vital, affecting fundamental truth, or where the offense constitutes a plain breach of morality (I Cor. 5:1-13; I Tim. 1:19, 20)" (Harvey).

The reason for the attitude lies in what the man is. "Knowing that" means that his refusal to listen to the admonitions administered has shown Titus what the man is. As to his character he is shown to be "perverted." The tense of the verb (perfect passive) indicates that he is in a state of being twisted, turned out of the right way. His refusal to heed the admonition shows that his is not so much an error of the mind as of the heart. As to his conduct, he "sinneth," goes on sinning, both by his factiousness and his refusal to listen to admonition. This leaves him guilty, "being self-condemned." He may not be conscious of his condemnation, but by his actions he unconsciously passes adverse judgment upon himself.

THE CONCLUSION, 3:12-15

The conclusion, comparable in length to the opening salutation, is devoted largely to personal matters (vv. 12-14). The closing verse contains the usual expression of greetings and a brief benediction (v. 15).

> When I shall send Artemas unto thee, or Tychicus, give diligence to come unto me to Nicopolis: for there I have determined to winter. Set forward Zenas the lawyer and Apollos on their journey diligently, that nothing be wanting unto them. And let our people also learn to maintain good works for necessary uses, that they be not unfruitful. All that are with me salute thee. Salute them that love us in faith. Grace be with you all.

1. The Personal Matters, vv. 12-14

Paul adds two matters of personal concern to Titus. He indicates his plans for the future movements of Titus (v. 12) and lays upon him the immediate obligation to assist Zenas and Apollos (v. 13). The thought of material assistance is next related more generally to the Cretan Christians (14).

a. The direction to Titus personally, v. 12. As his valued assistant, Paul indicates his further wishes for Titus. "When I shall send Artemas unto thee, or Tychicus, give diligence to come unto me to Nicopolis." These two fellow workers evidently were available as replacements for Titus on Crete. Artemas is not mentioned elsewhere, hence we have no information about this man. But it is clear that he was a trusted worker, in the same class with Tychicus and Titus. Tychicus was one of Paul's close associates about whom we have more information. He was a native of the province of Asia (Acts 20:4) and probably accompanied Paul to Jerusalem on the third missionary journey. During his first imprisonment in Rome, Paul chose him as the bearer of the Ephesian and Colossian epistles (Eph. 6:21; Col. 4:7). In the latter epistle Paul describes Tychicus as "the beloved brother and faithful minister and fellow servant in the Lord." From II Timothy 4:12 we learn that Paul sent him on a subsequent mission to Ephesus.

As the indefinite clause in the original (*hotan* with the subjunctive) indicates, Paul had not yet determined when either of the two men would be dispatched to Crete. Titus would of course remain at his post until the replacement arrived, as "unto thee" informs him. Paul requests Titus to rejoin him at Nicopolis. There were a number of cities named Nicopolis ("city of victory"), but the city here intended is evidently the one on the Ambracian Gulf in Epirus, built by Augustus to commemorate the battle of Actium. Paul explains why he wants Titus to meet him there, "for there I have determined to winter." The "there" shows that Paul was not yet at Nicopolis when he wrote. Just where Paul was when he wrote the letter to Titus we do not know, perhaps in Achaia or Macedonia. The statement of Paul's plans for the winter show that he was at liberty at the time. It is another indication that this Epistle was written after the release from the first Roman imprisonment.

It is obvious that Paul expected one of the two men mentioned to replace Titus on Crete. The position of Titus on Crete was not permanent. He was not the "first bishop of the Cretans" as the subscription, added to some copies of the Epistle, asserts. Titus was working on Crete as the apostle's personal representative, and his presence there did not alter the organizational setup in the local churches on Crete.

b. The instructions concerning Zenas and Apollos, v. 13. In this verse we get a glimpse of Paul as a great spiritual general moving his workers into strategic positions. And Titus is to have a part in furthering that work. "Set forward Zenas the lawyer and Apollos on their journey diligently, that nothing be wanting unto them." They are on a journey, perhaps under the guidance of Paul, which will take them by Crete. They have brought the letter to Titus. Now Titus is to "set them forward" on their journey. He is to give diligence to see that their needs for the journey are supplied. This matter of assisting Christian workers on their journey is mentioned in different places by Paul (Rom. 15:24; I Cor. 16:6, 11; II Cor. 1:16).

Of Zenas we know nothing further, and even the description of him as "the lawyer" leaves it uncertain whether the designation is Jewish or Roman. If the term is used with the same meaning it has in the Gospels, then he was a Jewish Christian who had been an expert in Jewish law and the designation continued to be applied to him by his Christian friends. Since his name is Greek, it may well be that he is or was a practitioner of Roman law and is now using his abilities in the interest of the Gospel. If so, he is the only Christian lawyer mentioned in the Bible.

Apollos was the eloquent preacher from Alexandria whom Aquila and Priscilla instructed more fully in the way of the Lord at Ephesus. His subsequent work at Corinth was with great power (Acts 18:24-28). His abilities made his name a rallying point for the party spirit at Corinth which Paul had to rebuke (I Cor. 1:12-4:6). Later he became an associate of Paul in work (I Cor. 16:12). This reference shows that there was no jealousy in the heart of Paul for the popular orator, nor was there any real opposition between their teaching.

c. The instructions concerning the Cretan Christians, v. 14. While Titus is told personally to see that these two missionary workers have their needs supplied, Paul here implies that Titus will turn to the local congregation for the needs of these men. Thus Hervey concludes: "The natural inference is that Titus had some fund at his disposal with which he was to help the travelers, but that St. Paul wished the Cretan Christians to contribute also." At any rate, this would give Titus a good opportunity to cultivate in the Cretan Christians this missionary spirit. This and similar opportunities would give them an opportunity to practice Christian giving, thus learning "to maintain good works for necessary uses." This is needful not only for the furtherance of the Gospel but also for the spiritual welfare of the Christians. The result contemplated is, "that they be not unfruitful." If they do not step forward with active good works when such occasions arise, they will scarcely learn how to do other good works. "Christianity which does not involve generosity and self-denial in the most ordinary ways is apt to become a barren profession" (Brown).

Notice that Paul says "our people *also.*" This is an injunction that holds for believers everywhere. That pastor who does not give his people an opportunity for good works in such matters does his people and the church a great injustice.

2. The Salutations, v. 15a

The customary greetings are added. "All that are with me" means Paul's fellow workers at the time of writing. Paul does not name them since Zenas and Apollos would orally inform Titus about the group. And Titus is to pass on these greetings to "them that love us in faith." As true believers the Cretan Christians loved Paul and his associates. Their love bound them together. And this love operated in the sphere of faith. Those holding to the true faith loved Paul; the heretics did not.

The statement of the salutation is unique. It is another

argument for the Pauline authorship, since a forger would be unlikely to introduce unfamiliar features.

3. The Benediction, v. 15b

"Grace be with you all." The "you" is plural and includes all the Cretan Christians to whom Titus will convey Paul's greetings. It may well be that this Epistle would be read in the various churches, since a message from the apostle would be of interest to all. Paul closes on the note of grace which has been stressed in the letter. May our experience of the free, unmerited favor of God in Christ Jesus impel us to live lives which reveal His grace and love to others!

Bibliography on Titus

ALFORD, HENRY. *The Greek Testament.* Vol. III. London: Rivingtons (2nd ed., 1857), pp. 117, 416.

BERNARD, J. H. "The Pastoral Epistles," *Cambridge Greek Testament.* Cambridge: Cambridge University Press (1922), pp. lxxviii and 192.

BOISE, JAMES ROBINSON. *Notes, Critical and Explanatory on the Greek Text of Paul's Epistles.* Ed. NATHAN E. WOOD. Boston: Silver, Burdett & Co. (1896), p. 582.

BROWN, ERNEST FAULKNER. "The Pastoral Epistles," *Westminster Commentaries.* London: Methuen & Co. Ltd. (1917), pp. xxxiv and 121.

GREENE, J. P. "The Pastoral Epistles, First and Second Timothy, Titus," *The Convention Series.* Nashville, Tenn.: Sunday School Board, Southern Baptist Convention (1915), p. 210.

HARVEY, H. "Commentary on the Pastoral Epistles, First and Second Timothy and Titus; and the Epistle to Philemon," *An American Commentary on the New Testament.* Philadelphia: The American Baptist Publication Society (1890; reprint, no date), p. 164.

HERVEY, A. C. "Titus," *The Pulpit Commentary.* Grand Rapids: Wm. B. Eerdmans Publishing Co. (1950 reprint), p. 60.

HORTON, R. F. "The Pastoral Epistles," *The Century Bible.* London: Blackwood, Le Bas & Co. (no date), p. 196.

HUMPHREYS, A. E. "The Epistles to Timothy and Titus," *The Cambridge Bible for Schools.* Cambridge: Cambridge University Press (1925 reprint), p. 271.

HUTHER, JOH. ED. "Critical and Exegetical Handbook to the Epistles of St. Paul to Timothy and Titus," *Meyer's Critical and Exegetical Commentary on the New Testament.* Translated by DAVID HUNTER. Edinburgh: T. & T. Clark (1893), p. 379.

LENSKI, R. C. H. *The Interpretation of St. Paul's Epistles to the Colossians, to the Thessalonians, to Timothy, to Titus and to Philemon*. Columbus, Ohio: Lutheran Book Concern (1937), p. 986.

LILLEY, J. P. "The Pastoral Epistles," *Handbooks for Bible Classes*. Edinburgh: T. & T. Clark (1901), p. 255.

LIPSCOMB, DAVID. *A Commentary on the New Testament Epistles*. Vol. V. Ed., with additional notes, J. W. SHEPHERD. Nashville, Tenn.: Gospel Advocate Co. (1942), p. 324.

LOCK, WALTER. "A Critical and Exegetical Commentary on the Pastoral Epistles," *The International Critical Commentary*. Edinburgh: T. & T. Clark (1924; reprint 1936), pp. xliv and 163.

POPE, R. MARTIN. *The Epistles of Paul the Apostle to Timothy and Titus*. London: Charles H. Kelly (1901), p. 248.

SCOTT, E. F. "The Pastoral Epistles," *The Moffatt New Testament Commentary*. London: Hodder and Stoughton (1948 reprint), pp. xxxviii and 186.

SPENCE, H. D. M. "The Pastoral Epistles of St. Paul," *Ellicott's Commentary on the Whole Bible*. Vol. VIII. Grand Rapids: Zondervan Publishing House (reprint, no date), pp. 171-264.

VAN OOSTERZEE, J. J. "The Epistle of Paul to Titus," *Lange's Commentary on the Holy Scriptures*. Grand Rapids: Zondervan Publishing House (1950 reprint), p. 24.

WHITE, NEWPORT J. D. "The First and Second Epistles to Timothy and the Epistle to Titus," *The Expositor's Greek Testament*. Vol. IV. Grand Rapids: Wm. B. Eerdmans Publishing Co. (reprint, no date), pp. 55-202.

WUEST, KENNETH S. *The Pastoral Epistles in the Greek New Testament for the English Reader*. Grand Rapids: Wm. B. Eerdmans Publishing Co. (1952), p. 209.

THE EPISTLE TO PHILEMON

An Introduction to Philemon

THE BRIEF LETTER to Philemon is unique among the writings of Paul which have come down to us. It throws an interesting light upon the social operations of the Gospel. It presents a vivid picture of the Spirit of Christ at work on the baneful institution of human slavery. The story behind the letter has its roots deep in this evil institution as an integral part of Roman society. The condition of the vast hordes of slaves in the Roman Empire was degraded, and depressing in the extreme. Although slavery was accepted without question as an indispensable element of the structure of society, the moral effects of such an institution upon both slave and master were tragic indeed. This masterly note to Philemon reveals the operation of Christ's redeeming love as the true power for the amelioration and ultimate abolition of this tragic situation.

The occasion for the writing of this note to a friend by Paul was the return of the fugitive slave Onesimus to his master Philemon at Colossae (Col. 4:8, 9; Philemon 12). Under the providence of God, Onesimus had become converted at Rome through the instrumentality of Paul. Having become a Christian, he was now returning to his Christian master under the protective care of Tychicus, whom Paul was sending to Colossae with the epistle to that church.

Philemon is one of the "Prison Epistles" written by Paul at Rome during the imprisonment mentioned in Acts 28. The letter is contemporaneous with the Epistles to the Ephesians and the Colossians. Both were taken to their destination by Tychicus at the same time (Eph. 6:21, 22; Col. 4:7, 8). The date may be given as the summer of A.D. 62.

The purpose of the apostle in writing to Philemon was to assure his friend of the writer's high regard for him and to induce him to receive, forgive, and reinstate Onesimus. Paul's skillful execution of the difficult task of securing a reconciliation between an offended master and an offending but now penitent and transformed slave presents a masterpiece of Christian tact and spiritual wisdom.

The letter was sent with Tychicus and Onesimus on their joint journey to Colossae. Whether Tychicus or Onesimus himself delivered the letter is not indicated. Since Onesimus was being returned to Philemon under the care of Tychicus, it seems more probable that Tychicus, in personally delivering Onesimus to Philemon, would also present Philemon with this appeal from the apostle Paul.

An Outline of Philemon

I. THE SALUTATION, vv. 1-3
1. The Writer, v. 1a
2. The Readers, vv. 1b, 2
   a. The addressee: Philemon, v. 1b
   b. The associates, v. 2
3. The Greeting, v. 3

II. THE THANKSGIVING, vv. 4-7
1. The Nature of the Thanksgiving, v. 4
2. The Cause of the Thanksgiving, v. 5
3. The Contents of the Prayer for Philemon, v. 6
4. The Basis for the Thanksgiving, v. 7

III. THE APPEAL, vv. 8-21
1. The Preparation for Making the Appeal, vv. 8-16
   a. The one making the appeal, vv. 8, 9
      1) His attitude, vv. 8, 9a
      2) His position, v. 9b
   b. The person for whom the appeal is made, vv. 10, 11
      1) His relation to Paul, v. 10
      2) His transformed personality, v. 11
   c. The action of Paul in the case, vv. 12-14
      1) The action stated, v. 12a
      2) The action interpreted, vv. 12b-14
   d. The suggestion of providential overruling, vv. 15, 16

An Outlined Interpretation of Philemon

I. THE SALUTATION, vv. 1-3

> Paul, a prisoner of Christ Jesus, and Timothy our brother, to Philemon our beloved and fellow worker, and to Apphia our sister, and to Archippus our fellow soldier, and to the church in thy house: grace to you and peace from God our Father and the Lord Jesus Christ.*

THE SALUTATION in this brief note to Philemon conforms to the epistolary practice of the day. It contains the usual three elements; namely, the writer, the reader, and the greeting. All of Paul's letters adhere to this form. Yet his use of this form of salutation is never merely conventional nor stereotyped. He expands and modifies each element of the salutation according to his intuitive sense of propriety under the circumstances.

1. The Writer, v. 1a

The writer of a letter in those days, contrary to our modern practice, began with his own name. The name of Paul at the beginning of this brief letter would at once arouse a keen interest in the heart of its recipient. It was a name that was fragrant with precious memories in the mind of Philemon and those of his household. Any message from him would be eagerly read.

To his name at the head of his letters Paul usually adds some descriptive title or designation, indicative of his position and authority. Quite frequently he describes himself as "an apostle of Christ Jesus." On occasion he

* The text used is that of the American Standard Version (1901).

calls himself "a servant of Jesus Christ." But in this note Paul properly omits all reference to his official authority (apostle) or distinctive position of service (servant) as not fitting in a private and friendly letter. He rather describes himself as a "prisoner of Christ Jesus." This is the only place where Paul employs this designation in the salutation.

Avoiding all mention of official authority, in this letter Paul assumes the position of a supplicant. As himself the Lord's bondsman he will plead for another bondsman whose story is the burden of this letter. In begging mercy for this bondsman he points to his own bonds. No less than six times in this brief letter does Paul make reference to his imprisonment (vv. 1, 9, 10, 13, 22, 23). These repeated references to his imprisonment would make a tremendous appeal to Philemon. "How could Philemon resist an appeal which was penned within prison walls and by a manacled hand?" (Lightfoot).

But the term is not used merely to arouse sympathy. It is descriptive of his true position. "A prisoner *of Christ Jesus*." (The order "Jesus Christ," followed in the King James Version, lacks manuscript authority.) There is a dignity and reverence about it. It is because of his relationship to Christ that he is a prisoner. The designation distinguishes him from a host of other prisoners who are held for reasons that have nothing to do with Christ. The world may consider him the prisoner of Nero, but Paul looks beyond secondary causes to recognize his Lord in it. His imprisonment is due not to any whimsical caprice on his part, still less because of any crime against the State, but solely because of his devoted attachment and unswerving loyalty to Christ. The appeal of one who was thus suffering for his Lord would not only arouse the sympathy of Philemon but would touch his conscience as well.

With his own name as writer, Paul associates that of "Timothy our brother." Paul not infrequently thus unites the name of an associate with his own in his letters. The naming of Timothy here does not mean that he assisted Paul in the composition of the letter. Nor does it prove that Paul dictated the letter to Timothy.

The addition of his name intimates that Timothy stood in complete agreement with Paul on the matter which occasioned the letter. Timothy is called "the brother" (Gr.). Apparently Timothy, like Paul himself, was well known to Philemon. Timothy appears to have been with Paul during the greater part of his three years' residence at Ephesus. It was at this time that he must have become acquainted with Philemon. Timothy as well as Paul was interested in the case of Onesimus. The addition of his name serves to add weight to the appeal. "A suit thus preferred and seconded could hardly fail to command respectful attention and favor at the outset" (Drysdale).

The designation of Timothy as "brother" would also remind Philemon of that great brotherhood of all believers into which he himself had been brought at his own conversion. It was this very spirit of brotherhood, engendered by faith in Christ, which Paul confidently expected to work a kindly reception for Onesimus in the heart of Philemon.

Timothy disappears from the letter following the mention of his name in the salutation. It is Paul himself who is carrying the appeal to Philemon. Throughout the letter the apostle speaks only in the first person singular. In Colossians the plural is maintained throughout the thanksgiving only.

2. The Readers, 1b, 2

If our identification of the people mentioned in the salutation is correct, this letter affords us a singular and interesting glimpse into a Christian household in New Testament times.

a. The addressee: Philemon, v. 1b

Although others are named in the salutation along with

Philemon, the letter is unmistakably directed to him. The second person *plural* pronoun, used in the greeting (v. 3), does not occur again until the conclusion (vv. 22, 25). The second person *singular* pronoun, having direct reference to Philemon himself, occurs no less than twenty times in this brief note. Twice Paul addresses him directly as "brother" (vv. 7, 20).

The name of Philemon does not occur elsewhere in the New Testament, although the name is not uncommon in Greek writings and inscriptions. He appears as the head of the household which is the recipient of this letter. He was a native, at least a resident, of the town of Colossae. This is evident from Paul's statements concerning Onesimus. In Colossians 4:9 Onesimus is said to belong to Colossae and was immediately returning there; here (v. 12) Paul informs Philemon that he is sending Onesimus back to him. Thus it is clear that Philemon made his home in Colossae.

From verse 19 it is evident that Philemon was a convert of the apostle Paul. Since Paul had not personally labored at Colossae (Col. 2:1), it seems probable that Philemon came into touch with Paul during the apostle's protracted stay at Ephesus and was converted there (Acts 19:10).

He seems to have been a man of prominent social standing and of some wealth. This is implied, not by the fact that he owned a slave, but from the fact that he had a house large enough to form a meeting place for Christians (v. 2), and especially from the reference to his liberality and hospitality which had been extended to brethren even from a distance (vv. 5-7).

That Philemon had endeared himself to both Paul and Timothy is evident from Paul's expression "our beloved." (In the Greek the word "our" may quite properly be taken to refer to both "beloved" and "fellow worker.") Both writers knew a sincere love for him. The character of Philemon, as shadowed forth in this Epistle, presents a noble picture, eminently worthy of the apostle's love and esteem.

"Our fellow worker" indicates the reason for this love. Their labors in a common cause bound them together. Where they had labored together is not stated. But the title is a noble testimony to the evangelistic zeal of Philemon. The term "fellow worker" is applied to ministers (II Cor. 8:23; Phil. 2:25; Col. 4:11), but it is not restricted to them (Rom. 16:3). It need not imply that Philemon was an official in the church at Colossae. But according to his station and ability Philemon worked in the same cause so dear to the heart of Paul.

b. The associates, v. 2

Two other individuals and a group of believers are associated with Philemon in the salutation. "And to Apphia our sister, and to Archippus our fellow soldier, and to the church in thy house."

It is commonly assumed that Apphia was the wife of Philemon. The position of her name between that of two active Christians implies her close relation to Philemon; otherwise her name would have been placed after that of Archippus.

Paul's designation of her as "our sister" shows that she too was a Christian and thus in sympathy with Philemon. As the wife of Philemon she naturally would have a definite interest in the return of Onesimus and would influence the decision of her husband in the case. As one who likewise has the furtherance of the cause of Christ at heart, Paul appeals to her "to take a Christian and enlightened interest in the matters that affect a church or household's credit and well-being" (Drysdale).

The reading in the King James Version, "to our beloved Apphia," rests on a different and inferior reading. "Our sister" is the reading supported by a preponderance of ancient authority and suits the context best. This read-

ing "preserves the line of thought in the sentence, balanc-
ing the epithets 'fellow-worker,' 'fellow-soldier,' applied
to Philemon and Archippus" (Wm. Alexander). It would
be somewhat inconsistent for Paul to introduce a mere
touch of emotional feeling in a clause apparently con-
structed for a different purpose.

To that of Philemon and Apphia Paul adds the name
of Archippus. This reference and Colossians 4:17 give all
that we know about him. The mention of his name here
implies that he was connected with the household of
Philemon. Just what that relation was cannot be positively established. A variety of surmises have been advanced. Some have taken him to be a *friend* of the household; others have regarded him as the *teacher* to the
household. More probable is the suggestion that he was
the *brother* of Philemon who made his home there. The
usual suggestion is that Archippus was the *son* of Philemon. If so, then Philemon must have been a man of
nearly Paul's own age.

Paul's description of Archippus as "our fellow soldier"
is a gracious compliment to this Christian worker. It implies that he has shown himself an aggressive soldier in
the battle for the Lord. Just where he had been engaged
in spiritual campaigns with the apostle is not known, but
perhaps while Paul was laboring at Ephesus. At any rate,
it is expressive of Paul's appreciation and approval of the
ministry Archippus is carrying on in Colossae. The picture of the Christian life as a warfare is common to the
writings of Paul. It may have been stimulated by his environment at the time that these "Prison Epistles" were
written. The picture is apt, for the whole Christian life,
then as well as now, was a continuing conflict.

From Colossians 4:17 it is sometimes assumed that
Archippus was engaged in a ministry at Laodicea. But his
mention here as part of the household of Philemon
clearly places him in Colossae. However, the proximity of

the two cities makes it not unlikely that he may have ministered in both places. It would seem that Archippus was active in pastoral responsibilities. The departure of Epaphras for Rome had placed special responsibilities upon his shoulders for the work there in the Lycus valley.

By means of the epithets employed Paul tactfully recognizes both Philemon and Archippus as comrades in Christian activity, the one in toil, the other in the ranks of battle. Although he is now "a *prisoner* of Christ Jesus," he yet claims the right to stand with them as a *laborer* and a *soldier*.

The salutation is made to include, further, "the church in thy house." The singular pronoun "thy" has reference to Philemon, and not to Archippus. It pays honor to Philemon as the head of his own household.

Two interpretations have been given to the phrase "the church in thy house." Chrysostom, Theodoret, and others thought that Paul thereby intended to designate the slaves and other members of Philemon's household. The more probable and generally accepted view is that Paul has in view "the section of the Christians at Colossae which met in his house" (Meyer). This would include such slaves in Philemon's household as were Christians. Under this interpretation Philemon is reminded that the matter of his actions concerning Onesimus is not strictly a private affair. Although he will be the sole legal arbiter in the case, he cannot forget that, as a member of a larger spiritual community, his dealings with Onesimus will be of vital concern to them all. His treatment of Onesimus will have abiding significance for the group. It was in that spiritual circle that a pardoned and restored Onesimus would have to find his place at Colossae. It is indicative of the tact of the apostle that he includes yet keeps within the limits of Philemon's family and religious circles when writing to him about this domestic problem.

The gathering of this company of believers in the house

of Philemon is characteristic of the time. Lightfoot asserts: "There is no clear example of a separate building set apart for Christian worship within the limits of the Roman empire before the third century" (on Col. 4:15). Christian congregations were dependent upon the hospitality of wealthy members who could furnish their own houses for this purpose. This note thus contains an indication of the social status of Philemon. In a large city there would be several such assemblies. (Cf. Rom. 16:5, 10, 11, 14, 15.) Whether the church at Colossae had more than one place of assembly is not known. Probably they did.

It has been suggested that we owe the preservation of this beautiful little letter to the fact that it was addressed to a congregational circle as well as to a private individual. Certainly it must be only one of numerous such private letters which Paul penned in the prosecution of his manifold apostolic labors.

3. The Greeting, v. 3

The greeting is in a form familiar from Paul's other writings. "Grace to you and peace from God our Father and the Lord Jesus Christ." The "you" is in the plural and includes all those who have been named.

For Paul these words are vastly more than a mere conventional greeting. They are in reality a fervent wish or prayer for the readers. In this private letter Paul uses the same greeting he uses in his public and didactic letters; it lifts at once this whole affair into the very presence of God and sanctifies it with the name of the Lord. The greeting as formulated indicates both the scope of the apostle's loving wish and the source to which he looks for its fulfillment.

The nature of the desired blessing is "grace . . . and peace." They comprise Heaven's choicest blessings. "Grace" is the free, unmerited favor of God through which salvation is bestowed upon the lost. It reminds us of our sins and speaks of their forgiveness by an infinite compassion. "Peace" is the result of the reception of the grace of God. It expresses the outcome of a right relationship between God and man brought about through grace. The former designates the source of salvation, while the latter speaks of the result of salvation in subjective experience. The order in the salutations is always "grace and peace," never the reverse. We cannot know the peace without first receiving the grace.

The source to which Paul looks for the fulfillment of this wish is indicated in the words "from God our Father and the Lord Jesus Christ." The blessings derive from a double source. They come from Him who holds the relationship of Father to all believers because of their union with His Son. They also come from the Son who is given the authoritative position of Lord in the lives of believers. The union of the two under the government of the one preposition "from" is indicative of Paul's faith in the equality of the Father and the Son and the identity of the operations proceeding from both. As one who was steeped in the Hebrew revelation of the unity of God, for Paul to have united the name of Jesus with that of God, if he thought Him but a man, would have been blasphemy.

Here was the unfailing source of grace and peace upon which Philemon would needs draw in settling aright the problem about to be presented to him. "Looking to this Source every believer may be assured of limitless supplies of 'grace' and the enjoyment of a 'peace' that passes all understanding" (Erdman).

II. THE THANKSGIVING, vv. 4-7

I thank my God always, making mention of thee in my prayers, hearing of thy love, and of the faith which thou hast toward the Lord Jesus, and toward all the saints; that the fellowship of thy faith may become effectual, in the knowledge of every good thing which is in you, unto

Christ. For I had much joy and comfort in thy love, because the hearts of the saints have been refreshed through
thee, brother.

As usual in the Pauline writings, the apostle begins
this letter with a paragraph of thanksgiving and intercession. This practice reveals the habitual devoutness of
his spirit. The exceptions are II Corinthians, where Paul
writes under great emotional strain because of the petty
suspicions and unfounded charges of his Corinthian
enemies, and Galatians, where a vehement denunciation
of their fickleness takes the place of the usual thanksgiving. These exceptions prove that Paul's practice of
thanksgiving for his readers was not a mere formality but
rather the natural and sincere expression of his feelings
at the time of writing.

Wisely Paul does not at once plunge into a presentation
of the matter which was the occasion for this letter. In
this paragraph he tactfully begins with a heartfelt expression of his own high esteem for Philemon. His first
move is to pour out his own heart to his friend. Joy and
thanksgiving warm his heart as he thinks of the good reports he is hearing about Philemon. What he knows
about Philemon gives added incentive to the writing of
the letter. Paul would not have Philemon think that he is
writing simply because of Onesimus. "He assigns other
causes also of his Epistle. In the first place manifesting
his love, then also desiring that a lodging may be prepared for him" (Chrysostom).

1. The Nature of the Thanksgiving, v. 4

The opening verse of this paragraph describes the
nature of Paul's thanksgiving. It is Godward, personal,
and continual.

The reports about Philemon do not merely fill him
with a sense of gratitude but lead him to a definite expression of thanksgiving to God. Paul followed the com-
mendable practice of immediately lifting everything

which came into his life up to God in thanksgiving and prayer. As Christians we too need to exercise this practice of consciously bringing every circumstance in our life before the Lord. Such a practice of the presence of God is of inestimable value for victorious living.

The thanksgiving is personal. "*I* thank *my* God." Paul knew God in personal experience. Paul was conscious of a vital personal relationship with God. "In speaking of God as *my* God, he expresses a tender sense of his reconciliation to Him, and of his consciousness of an interest in His love" (Hackett). God was a vital reality to him, and Paul instinctively turned to Him in joy as well as in sorrow. It is the privilege of every believer to approach God as his own God. But this personal thanksgiving was stimulated by Paul's recognition of the grace of God in the life of Philemon. This manifestation of God's grace in the life of his convert Paul thankfully accepted as a gift bestowed upon himself.

The thanksgiving is continual. This is indicated by the use of the present tense of the verb which expresses the action as continuing. This fact is further emphasized by the addition of the word "always." Grammatically it may be joined either with the following participle (as in the King James) or with the opening verb (as in the American Standard Version). The latter view is preferable as more in accord with Paul's practice elsewhere. "But it is of comparatively small moment how we place the word, provided we observe that Paul's prayer as an exercise of devotion or praise to God, precedes his prayer as an exercise of desire for man" (Drysdale). Paul's sense of thanksgiving is not exhausted by a single expression of thanks; repeatedly he finds himself giving thanks to God for Philemon.

Paul's thanksgiving is exercised upon the occasion of his prayers. "Making mention of thee in my prayers." These constant thanks for Philemon are offered in the course of Paul's regular prayer periods. Here we get a glimpse of the great prayer ministry of the apostle. Paul's practice of praying for the readers of his epistles is well known. "So broad was his spiritual sympathy, that he daily spread out before God the condition and needs of the multitude of churches and of fellow laborers, with whom he was connected as spiritual leader, evidently mentioning them by name, and entering into their circumstances and special necessities with great particularity" (Harvey). How often the names found in his epistles must have been upon his lips in prayer! In this intercessory ministry Philemon has a definite place.

2. The Cause of the Thanksgiving, v. 5

The thanksgiving for Philemon is occasioned by the good reports which Paul is hearing about him. The use of the present tense indicates that the subject is continually present in conversation. This information about Philemon doubtless came to him from Epaphras, now with Paul at Rome (v. 23; Col. 1:7, 8). Perhaps other believers present who were acquainted with Philemon added to the reports. The information which Onesimus could give would hardly be recent and could only represent the impressions of one who was an outsider at the time. Doubtless Onesimus expressed his impressions of Philemon viewed in the light of his recent experience.

The contents of these gratifying reports is indicated thus: "Hearing of thy love, and of the faith which thou hast toward the Lord Jesus, and toward all the saints." This ambiguous sentence has been differently understood. The confusion seems largely to have been caused by the unusual order of the wording of the sentence. Paul begins by saying that he hears about the dual subject of Philemon's love and faith (the position of "thy" in the original indicates that it belongs to both nouns); but the order of the wording in the relative clause does not seem to correspond to this dual subject. This apparent discrepancy has led to the changed order "thy faith and love" in a few minor manuscripts, corresponding to the order in Colossians 1:4. But this order is unwarranted by the best manuscripts and is obviously an emendation. Some scholars, like Meyer and Beet, accepting the true order of the words, seek to obviate the difficulty by applying the entire relative clause to "faith" (*pistis*), interpreted to mean "faithfulness" rather than "faith." That *pistis* does have this meaning in the New Testament, although rarely, is true. But that this is the meaning of the word here is doubtful. In the New Testament the expression "to have faith" never means "to have faithfulness." Further, when faith and love are used together in the New Testament, "faith" always has its ordinary theological meaning. The fact that Paul here mentions love before faith does not invalidate the assertion. Love is ever the fruit of faith; the relation remains the same regardless of the order used. This view also leaves "thy love" without any specified object to which the love is directed. It is best to retain the ordinary meaning for "faith" here.

As it stands the sentence is a good illustration of the impetuous style of Paul, words tumbling over each other in the rush of thoughts seeking to find expression. Most commentators regard the order of the words as in effect an example of the grammatical figure called *chiasm,* that is, a crossing up like the letter X. An example of *chiasm* would be: "The blind and the dumb spake and saw," meaning, "The blind saw; the dumb spake." That Paul intended the two nouns "love and faith" to be taken together is evident from the place of "thy" before both in the original. The following relative clause refers to both nouns, the relative pronoun (in the singular) being in accord with the nearest substantive. But the two prepositional phrases, "toward the Lord Jesus, and toward all the saints," stand in a crosswise relation to love and faith. The arrangement of the phrases, on this view, is admittedly strange. Yet this distribution is strengthened by the fact that in Colossians 1:4, written at the same time, the terms in question are so distributed without ambiguity. So also in Ephesians 1:15. Paul's use of two different prepositions (*pros* and *eis*), apparently in a desire to separate the two clauses, seems further confirmation of this view.

Lightfoot explains the order of the words in the sentence as due to "the apostle's setting down the thoughts in the sequence in which they occur to him, without paying regard to symmetrical arrangement. The first and prominent thought is Philemon's love. This suggests the mention of his faith, as the source from which it springs. This again requires a reference to the object of faith. And then at length comes the deferred sequel to the first thought—the range and comprehensiveness of his love." The very structure of the sentence reminds us of the fact that genuine love and faith are closely knit together in actual operation.

Love is the fruit or result of faith. Paul places love first as the prominent thought. "Love toward the saints" includes the brother for whom he will plead; the case of Onesimus will be a test of Philemon's Christian love, hence Paul's thought puts it in the foreground.

Paul cannot forget for a moment that Christian love springs from faith in the Lord Jesus. He knows that the essence of the Christian life is "faith working through love" (Gal. 5:6). "The source and foundation of goodness and nobility of character is faith in Jesus the Lord" (Maclaren). The designation "the Lord Jesus" speaks of the Divine-human nature of Him who is the object of faith. Christian faith sees and accepts both the divinity and humanity in Him. Both are essential for saving faith. A faith which grasps only the humanity of Jesus has no basis for the hope of salvation, since a mere man cannot redeem men (Ps. 49:7). But the faith which sees the splendor and infinite holiness of God incarnate in Jesus Christ finds a sure basis of salvation in the mediatory work of Him who is both God and man. Christian faith has a full-orbed view of Him who is the object of faith and service. Philemon's faith is said to be "toward (*pros*) the Lord Jesus." The preposition pictures that faith as turned toward the Lord Jesus in glory and stretching out in longing aspiration toward Him.

But Philemon's faith in the Lord Jesus was no mere empty sentiment or profession; it found active expression in his love "toward (*eis*) all the saints." The change of prepositions indicates "a delicate distinction between the physical nearness of saints, on whom may be poured forth the tokens of love in visible and tangible form, and the physical remoteness of the Lord Jesus, whom we cannot thus locally reach" (Drysdale). Philemon has shown himself to be a benefactor of the brotherhood. The recipients of his benefactions are called "saints." It is the common New Testament designation for all believers, not just those who have attained to a superior degree of piety. It pictures them as those who have been "set apart," or "consecrated," to the service of God. Their consecration to a holy God naturally implies a holy character consistent with such consecration. Yet the designation is used of those who in actual practice fall short of the ideal. In I Corinthians 1:2 Paul applies it to the Corinthians although he found it necessary severely to condemn their conduct. It refers to the normal or prescribed standard of Christian character, although in actual experience believers only too often fail to realize the implied standard of holiness in the name—"Ye shall be holy; for I am holy" (I Peter 1:16).

In this picture of Philemon's love toward all the saints Paul doubtless intends for him to understand that Onesimus is now included among them. He must allow his love to be operative toward him as well.

3. The Contents of the Prayer for Philemon, v. 6

Verse 5 was a parenthesis of thought. Verse 6 expounds the reference to Paul's prayers in verse 4. Paul not only thanks God for Philemon's love and faith but he also prays "that the fellowship of thy faith may become effectual, in the knowledge of every good thing which is in you, unto Christ." Paul is devoutly thankful for the blessings bestowed upon Philemon, but he cannot rest satisfied with them without asking for more. The very satisfaction which the cool, refreshing waters at the well afford the weary traveler makes him desirous to draw more largely on its abundant supply for himself and for others. Thus it is in the Christian life. The blessings already received from God by their very perfections make us sublimely discontented with our attainments in them and stir the desire for more.

In this verse we have Paul's formulation of the contents of his prayer for Philemon. It gives us the contents as well as the object of the apostle's intercession. It may well be regarded as an example of the customary private petitions which Paul is offering for Philemon at this time.

Paul's great desire for Philemon is that he may increase in knowledge as he grows in grace, that in the active and effectual exercise of the fellowship of his faith, he may apprehend more clearly and possess more fully and richly the full knowledge of every good thing which is the possession of the believer by virtue of his union with Christ, all of which will result in the glory of Christ.

Philemon's faith puts him into fellowship with the saints. This fellowship is first of all an inner spiritual relationship of all who truly believe in Christ. Out of this inner relationship flow those acts of love and brotherliness which characterize the Christian life. Paul prays that Philemon's faith may be active or energetic without a break (constative aorist). His faith is not to be passive or quiescent but actively operative in its relations to others, producing good fruit. The apostle's desire is that this fellowship may be operative in the sphere of a full knowledge, "the knowledge of every good thing which is in you." It is a knowledge "which comes by actual possession of every grace of experience and character which is made possible to us by the new spiritual nature that, through God's gift, is in us" (Harvey). It involves the complete appropriation of all God-given truth and unreserved personal identification with the known will of God. This knowledge is the reward of faith manifesting itself in deeds of love. Such a knowledge of every good thing that is in reality the present possession of the believer certainly implies an extraordinary advance in his spiritual life. It is the goal of full-orbed spiritual maturity.

And all of this is to be "unto Christ." (It is rightly set off by a comma as relating to this entire verse.) The Christian life with all of its achievements, all development of character, is unto the glory of Christ, for His praise and honor. Such is the aim of the true life of grace.

Although this prayer is quite broad and generally stated, from the contents of the letter it is clear that in the formulation of it Paul had Onesimus in mind. The more Philemon comes to see these good things in other believers the less will he be inclined to take amiss the request of Paul. He "will not allow his resentment toward Onesimus to prevent his recognizing the good which the knowledge of Christ has developed in him" (Vincent). His action of forgiveness and love to Onesimus will be a means of deepening his own experience of these good things.

4. The Basis for the Thanksgiving, v. 7

In concluding this paragraph of thanksgiving the apostle indicates the subjective ground for the thanksgiving described in verse four. It was based on the love of Philemon as expressed in his ministries of beneficence to the saints.

Paul is still speaking for himself alone. The reading in the King James Version, "For we have . . ." rests upon inferior manuscript authority. In verse 4 he used the present tense of continuing action; here he employs the tense of point action (aorist) to emphasize the immediate reaction that the news of Philemon's active love produced in him. This he describes as having been "much joy and comfort." "The news of Philemon's love had animated the apostle" (Moule). It had sent a beam of happiness into his dreary imprisonment and had given him encouragement in his bondage. "The secret of all this 'joy and consolation' is found in his spirit of mingled gratitude and benevolence. A thankless heart has no security for any abiding joy and consolation" (Drysdale).

But the love which thus stimulated the apostle was directed not to himself but to others. It gladdened his own heart because it refreshed the hearts of the saints. He finds himself rested and soothed with those who find rest under Philemon's roof. He rejoices to record that "the saints have been refreshed" by the love-inspired ministries of Philemon. Just what these ministries were we are not informed. Doubtless Epaphras informed Paul about them. That they were bestowed upon the saints which met in Philemon's house seems obvious. But it may well be that these ministries were not limited to the saints at Colossae; they may well have extended to missionary friends from other places whom Philemon entertained in his home or forwarded on their journeys. Their contacts with Philemon caused them to experience a definite refreshment of heart which issued in fresh energies for further labors for the Lord. Paul is happy to record that this has been accomplished "through thee." Philemon has proved himself the agent for his Lord in so doing.

What an interesting chain of happy influences this paragraph presents! Philemon's faith in Christ has inspired a love for the saints which has manifested itself in active beneficence to the saints which has cheered and encouraged them for further service. The report of this fact, wafted as a breath of refreshing air to Paul's prison, has stirred a glow of joy and encouragement in Paul's own heart and this in turn has inspired him to pray for Philemon that a richer experience of all Christian good might flow back into the life of Philemon. Such are the far-reaching influences of good deeds, motivated by Christian love.

The paragraph begins and ends upon the note of grateful thanksgiving for the nobleness of Philemon's character. It provides a wonderful atmosphere in which to present his request for Onesimus. But it is not done merely as a means of calculated diplomacy but is the result of instinctive kindness. Paul's heart goes out in genuine love for Philemon as he writes, as evidenced by the concluding word, "brother." This epithet, by its unusual position at the end of the sentence, "assumes the character of a sudden irrepressible shoot of love from Paul's heart toward Philemon, like the quick impulse with which a mother will catch up her child, and cover it with caresses" (Maclaren). It is an acknowledgment that in all these matters Philemon has shown himself a true brother to Paul, and in that consciousness the apostle can now present to him the matter of his spiritual child Onesimus.

III. THE APPEAL, vv. 8-21

Wherefore, though I have all boldness in Christ to enjoin thee that which is befitting, yet for love's sake I rather beseech, being such a one as Paul the aged, and now a prisoner also of Christ Jesus: I beseech thee for my child, whom I have begotten in my bonds, Onesimus, who once was unprofitable to thee, but now is profitable to thee and to me: whom I have sent back to thee in his own person, that is, my very heart: whom I would fain have kept with me, that in thy behalf he might minister unto me in the bonds of the gospel: but without thy mind I would do nothing; that thy goodness should not be as of necessity, but of free will. For perhaps he was therefore parted *from thee* for a season, that thou shouldest have him forever; no longer as a servant, but more than a servant, a brother beloved, specially to me, but how much rather to thee, both in the flesh and in the Lord. If then thou countest me a partner, receive him as myself. But if he hath wronged thee at all, or oweth *thee* aught, put that to mine account; I Paul write it with mine own hand, I will repay it: that I say not unto thee that thou owest to me even thine own self besides. Yea, brother, let me have joy of thee in the Lord: refresh my heart in Christ. Having confidence in thine obedience I write unto thee, knowing that thou wilt do even beyond what I say.

In this paragraph, which is the very heart of the letter, Paul comes to grips with the delicate task which called forth its writing. But he does not at once blurt out his request. With consummate skill and Christian wisdom he carefully paves the way for the formal presentation of the request, even intimating its nature before he finally formulates it.

1. The Preparation for Making the Appeal, vv. 8-16

The apostle skillfully prepares the ground to assure a favorable reaction to his appeal. He begins with a touching reference to the one making the request (vv. 8, 9), depicts the one for whom it is being made (vv. 10, 11), explains his action in the case (vv. 12-14), and softens the entire unpleasant story by the suggestion of the over-ruling hand of Providence in the matter (vv. 15, 16).

a. The one making the appeal, vv. 8, 9

Paul properly begins with a description of the one making the appeal. First he indicates the attitude he is adopting, then he notes the position of the one presenting the request.

1) His attitude, (vv. 8, 9a). When the apostle decided to interpose on behalf of Onesimus, two avenues of approach lay open to him. He might use the tone of authority or he might adopt the method of persuasion. He resolved to use the latter. This decision was strengthened by his knowledge of the character of Philemon. The opening "wherefore" refers back to verse seven and assigns the reason for the method adopted. Philemon's active love assures him that his appeal will find ready acceptance.

"Though I have all boldness in Christ to enjoin thee that which is befitting." This participial clause, concessive in nature, indicates the attitude he might adopt. Because of their intimate relations, Paul's apostolic office, and the character of Philemon, he might frankly tell Philemon what he ought to do. "Boldness" is "frank and open speech, without hesitation or holding back due to a fear of offending the other person's susceptibilities" (Lenski). That Paul felt that he might have used such an approach without offense is a fine compliment to Philemon. This "boldness" Paul has "in Christ," exercised in virtue of his relation to Him. "It is only *in Christ,* and by his authority as an apostle, that he could claim to come between a slave and his master. Secular warrant for doing so he had none" (Eales). The case in hand was one where Paul might well use his authority to command "that which is befitting." For him authoritatively to direct Philemon to forgive and restore Onesimus would have been in the sphere of his authority; it would have been the right and proper thing, morally becoming and eminently Christian. "Thus Paul makes that, which he desires to obtain from Philemon, already to be felt as his *duty*" (Meyer).

But Paul deliberately prefers to use a higher appeal with Philemon. "Yet for love's sake I rather beseech." He waives his right as an apostle and makes his appeal on the basis of love. No limitation is attached to "the love."

Some would refer it to Philemon's love, mentioned in verses 5 and 7. Others interpret it of the mutual love of Paul and Philemon. More probable is the view that Paul is speaking of the principle of love as such which demands a deferential respect. Although Paul had a right to command a Christian course of action in the present case because of its importance for the cause of Christ, yet out of esteem for Philemon he will rather humbly request.

2) His position, v. 9b. Adopting the position of the intercessor, Paul makes a twofold reference to the one making the appeal. He is "such a one as Paul the aged, and now a prisoner also of Christ Jesus." He touches two points, his age and his imprisonment.

He calls himself "Paul the aged." He is the Lord's veteran. As "an old man" he has been in the work for a long time. From what we know about Paul he must have been around sixty years old at this time. That is not very old according to modern standards. But Paul had lived dangerously. A man who had been five times beaten with forty stripes save one, thrice beaten with rods, once stoned, thrice* suffered shipwreck, been a night and a day in the deep, in journeys often amid manifold perils, experiencing physical privations, enduring "a thorn in the flesh," a man upon whom had fallen the care of all the churches (II Cor. 11:23-28; 12:7)—such a man showed and felt the weight of the years. The entreaty of such a one could not be lightly thrust aside.

The margin of the American Standard Version reads "an ambassador," a reading strongly advocated by Lightfoot and others after him. The Greek words for "old man" and "ambassador" are nearly identical and were often written alike (except for accent), hence either translation is possible. Lightfoot felt that the parallel passage

* Since II Corinthians was written before Acts 27, he had already experienced four shipwrecks when Philemon was written.

in Ephesians 6:20 favored "ambassador" here. Viewed thus the term would be a quiet reminder of the dignity and authority of the one making the appeal; he was the Lord's envoy. But this view seems out of harmony with the context. The reference to his dignity as the Lord's "ambassador" would be a recurrence to that very motive of official authority which he has just disclaimed. The rendering "an old man" is to be preferred. Nor is such an appeal inconsistent with the fact that Philemon, if he were the father of Archippus, could himself not be much younger. The gentleman from Colossae had not lived the strenuous life which Paul had lived and would bear his years much more lightly than the apostle. The import of the fact that Paul had grown old in the service of their common Lord would not be lost on Philemon.

The further description of his position as "now a prisoner also of Christ Jesus" would make an even stronger appeal to Philemon. The very man through whom Philemon had come to know the Gospel (v. 19) was now in bonds because of his services for that Gospel. It reminded him of the fact that "the weakness of age was aggravated by the helplessness of bonds" (Moule). Paul's relations to Christ as His messenger had forged those bonds. How could Philemon refuse a request from one who had borne so much for the Master to whom they both belonged? "Who can suppose that Philemon uttered no cry or shed no tears, when he came to this part of the letter?" (S. Gentilis, quoted by Wm. Alexander).

b. The person for whom the appeal is made, vv. 10, 11.

Following this touching prelude the apostle discloses who is the individual on whose behalf he is making the appeal. He describes this person first in relation to himself and then asserts his transformed personality.

1) His relation to Paul, v. 10. Before he utters the name of Onesimus Paul employs two introductory phrases indicating his own relations to him. By placing the name

of Onesimus at the end of the sentence, a fact blurred by the order adopted in the King James, he softens the unfavorable connotations of the name for Philemon as much as possible. (Compare the similar position of the name Isaac in Gen. 22:2.) These two preceding phrases are like "two shields which effectually cover the hated name that must now at length be uttered: Onesimus" (Van Oosterzee).

Paul calls him "my child." The use of the possessive pronoun in the original is stronger: "my own child." Paul is the spiritual father of this child. As such he takes his place with Timothy, Titus, and Philemon himself (v. 19) in the family circle. The designation speaks of tender love. The description also has in it "the thought of immaturity: Onesimus is only a child as yet, and in this condition needs much tender care" (Lenski). The added phrase, "whom I have begotten in my bonds," describes the dark prison setting for the father's joy. "Thus for the third time Philemon is made to hear the clanking of the prisoner's chain" (Beet).

It is for this beloved child that Paul is pleading. The repetition of the verb "beseech" shows the intensity of the apostle's feeling. He assumes the position of the intercessor (*precator*) on behalf of the fugitive slave with his master, thus exercising on behalf of Onesimus the one privilege of a fugitive slave which the Roman law recognized. Although unable himself to appear with Onesimus, he claims for himself the right to intercede with the master for him.

2) His transformed personality, v. 11. Anticipating the emotional strain which the very name of Onesimus would raise in the breast of Philemon, Paul frankly acknowledges the grievous failure but points at once to the fact of his transformed personality. He recognizes that Onesimus "once was unprofitable to thee." Paul's knowledge of the past character of Onesimus would convince Phile-

mon that Onesimus had made a full revelation of his un-savory past to Paul. Paul's employment of the term "un-profitable" in description of that past is an illustration of the cloaking action of Christian love; he does not paint the sin of Onesimus any blacker than necessary.

The name of Onesimus means "profitable," or "help-ful." Formerly he had not lived up to the meaning of his name, but the Gospel had produced a transformation in him, causing him to exemplify its meaning. Paul makes a kindly play upon the name by the use of a synonym with two different prefixes: once he was "unserviceable" (ach-rēston) but now he is "well serviceable" (euchrēston). And that transformation has significance "to thee and to me." Paul puts Philemon's interest first but he assumes a joint interest in the matter. "In Onesimus Philemon has gained a brother in Christ: and Paul another son in the Gospel" (Beet). But the change has also a practical profit for both of them. Onesimus will now be a benefit to his master, since he will serve him better than before; he has already shown himself a benefit to Paul through the ministries rendered him in his imprisonment (v. 13).

c. The action of Paul in the case, vv. 12-14

Having informed Philemon of the transformation in the erstwhile fugitive, Paul announces that he is sending him back to his master. This action he interprets from the viewpoint of his own interest as well as from his high esteem for Philemon.

1) The action stated, v. 12a. "Whom I have sent back to thee." The Greek has the epistolary aorist, "I sent," a definite act on Paul's part; in it "the writer puts himself at the point of time when the correspondent is reading his letter" (Vincent). This action was in accord with the demands of the Roman law. Onesimus has accompanied the letter and is now at Colossae; perhaps he is standing in the very presence of his master as Philemon reads it. His willingness to return to his offended master shows

the genuineness of his conversion. Whether or not Onesimus himself presented the letter to Philemon is not indicated. Since he was returned to Colossae under the care of Tychicus (Col. 4:7-9), it would seem more probable that Tychicus himself presented it to Philemon as the best preparation for the reception of the returning slave.

The text of the King James Version, "thou therefore receive him," follows an inferior reading. Paul does not yet state that request. This request he delays until verse 17. What intervenes will still further pave the way for the formulation of the request. He still has much to say to Philemon concerning the one for whom he is entering his plea.

2) The action interpreted, vv. 12b-14. Paul interprets his act of returning Onesimus to Philemon from the point of view of his own interests in the matter as well as from his manly consideration for Philemon.

From the viewpoint of Paul's personal comfort and interest the return of Onesimus was not easy. It was difficult because of his deep affection for Onesimus. "Him, that is, my very heart." "Onesimus, the vagabond slave, has become so precious to the apostle that sending him away is like tearing the heart out of his own breast" (Erdman). What an amazing impression this must have made upon Philemon!

Further, the return of Onesimus was difficult for Paul because it meant the loss of his valued services to him in his imprisonment. He had even pondered the thought of retaining him as his personal attendant during the remainder of his imprisonment. His use of the imperfect (eboulomēn) pictures the decision as half-formed but abandoned because of other considerations. A warm attachment has sprung up between the two men and the kindly services of Onesimus would have been very welcome to him, since as a prisoner he was dependent upon the ministries of others. And as the servant of Philemon, the ministries of Onesimus would have been considered as "in thy behalf." Philemon himself would be eager to render such services to the Lord's prisoner if he himself were present. A fourth reference to his imprisonment reminds Philemon of the fact that they are "the bonds of the gospel." He is in bonds because he is a herald of the Gospel. His arrest at Jerusalem was caused by his outspoken proclamation of the Gospel of salvation for all alike through faith in Christ.

But as Paul thought of Philemon he deliberately checked his inclination to retain Onesimus. "Without thy mind I would do nothing." The resolution has been formed to send him back to his master. To have retained him for his own benefit without the knowledge of the master would make the benefit thus received from Philemon look as if it had been extorted. "Paul could not continue to use the servant's labors without the master's knowledge, and yet reckon them as favors shown him by the master himself" (Drysdale). Any good which Paul receives from Philemon must not even have the appearance of compulsion but must be the expression of his own free will. Therefore, out of consideration for his friend Philemon, he has sent the servant back. This principle of consideration for others here manifested by Paul is a factor of vital importance today for effective Christian leadership. Many are the difficulties which might be avoided if those in places of authority in Christian work would follow Paul's example in this.

Paul's decision to return Onesimus to his master must have been influenced by several considerations, although only his regard for Philemon is mentioned. To have thus harbored and detained a fugitive slave would have been a violation of Roman law. Paul was keenly sensitive to the scandal which Christianity might create if slaves should thus be encouraged to become fugitives. Paul realized that it was necessary for Onesimus himself to return to his master. He had repented of his sin but he needed to make restitution for the wrong done to his master.

d. The suggestion of providential overruling, vv. 15, 16

To soften the attitude of Philemon toward Onesimus still further Paul suggests the probability of the overruling hand of God in the matter as a fuller explanation of it. The suggestion is introduced with an explanatory "for." Many expositors regard this as an added reason why Paul decided not to retain Onesimus with him. Such an action might have meant the defeat of the very purpose for which God allowed him to leave. But it seems more probable that Paul's presentation of the suggestion of providential overruling in the matter is another link in the chain which he is forging for the kindly reception of Onesimus by Philemon. The indication of Paul's desire to retain Onesimus for his own benefit is only a minor digression (vv. 13, 14); the main train of thought is the kindly reception to be given the returning fugitive.

Paul introduces the suggestion of divine providence with a modest "perhaps." The providential purposes of God are veiled to men and even Paul can speak of them only tentatively. He will not be too sure of what God meant by such and such a thing, as some men are wont to be, as if they had private access to the secret councils of God. While God does have His purposes in everything, He alone can certainly declare that intention. Yet the outcome in this case seems clearly to warrant the interpretation of the overruling purpose of God in the matter. A decided declaration that it was the purpose of God that Onesimus should thus flee from his master would have grated harshly on the feelings of Philemon.

With the words, "he was parted from thee," Paul describes the fault and flight of Onesimus, but his choice of the word "parted" is full of tact and Christian consideration. He avoids the harsher word "fled." That would have awakened a feeling of resentment in Philemon and would have needlessly stressed the self-will of the now penitent slave. His choice of words is admirably suited to spare the feelings of both master and slave. It puts the offense of Onesimus as gently as human language can frame it. The use of the passive "was parted" may be intended to turn Philemon's attention from the individual wrong of Onesimus to the providence of God which made this wrong to work for good. Viewed thus it would be comparable to the experience of Joseph in being separated from his brethren (Gen. 45:5). However, since the usage of the verb is not strictly passive in meaning (a passive form with a deponent middle force) it may simply mean "departed," as in the King James translation.

Paul suggests that the separation was but "for a season, that thou shouldest have him forever." How long Onesimus had been gone we do not know; it probably had not been very long. But in the light of eternity the duration of the separation was but "for an hour" (Gr.). It was but brief in comparison to the magnitude of the change which had been wrought. "He departed a reprobate; he returns a saved man" (Lightfoot). As such Philemon will possess him forever. The compound form of the verb in the original denotes the completeness of the possession. "The bond between the master and the slave would no longer be that of ownership by purchase which death would dissolve, but their common relation to Christ which made them brethren, now and evermore" (Vincent).

Immediately following this suggestion that Onesimus should be received back fully in a new relationship, Paul spells out the nature of that relationship, "no longer as a servant, but more than a servant, a brother beloved, specially to me, but how much rather to thee, both in the flesh and in the Lord." These are striking words indeed. Onesimus may retain the position of a slave outwardly, may continue to be regarded as such in the eyes of the

Roman law, but for Philemon he has come to be much more than that, "a brother beloved." The common union of the master and the slave to Christ has placed them on a level of moral equality in the kingdom of God.

Paul claims Onesimus as "a brother beloved, specially to me." Philemon's beloved brother in the Lord was Paul's most beloved "child." Paul emphasizes his own love for Onesimus and then goes on to infer an even greater affection on the part of Philemon because of the double relationship, "in the flesh and in the Lord." The former denotes the external and civil relations where Onesimus will be a better servant; the latter denotes the spiritual sphere where he stands on a level of equality as a Christian brother. "In the flesh Philemon has the brother as a slave, and in the Lord the slave as a brother; how greatly, therefore, must he, in view of the mutual connection and interpenetration of the two relations, have him as a *beloved* brother!" (Meyer).

The reference to Onesimus as Philemon's brother "in the flesh" has raised the conjecture that Philemon and Onesimus were physically related, the latter being born of a slave mother, hence having the status of a slave. But Paul's use of the word "brother" affords no proof of such a natural relationship between Philemon and Onesimus.

Paul does not say a word against the institution of slavery as such. He does not interfere with the civil relationships, but he does deal with the moral and spiritual relationships. He does not say, "no longer a servant," but "no longer *as* a servant." He does not make a frontal attack on the inhuman institution; rather he injects the dynamic of Christian love and allows it to transform the conditions of temporal servitude into a holy brotherhood. It was this principle which effected the eventual abolition of slavery as a legal institution.

2. The Formulation of the Request, vv. 17-21

At length the apostle feels ready to formulate the request which seems to have been trembling on his lips since verse twelve. The broken structure in verse twelve finds its sequel in verse seventeen where the formal request is stated. The "then" (*oun*) of this verse summarizes the different considerations for the reception of Onesimus which have been advanced and enforce the formal statement of the plea with accumulative effect.

a. The statement of the request, v. 17

The long delayed request, already intimated in what has been said, is now formally stated: "If then thou countest me a partner, receive him as myself." Even now the apostle prefaces the words of the actual appeal with a powerful inducement, namely, Philemon's regard for Paul himself. "If thou countest me a partner." Paul's term "partner" must not be weakened to mean merely an intimate friend or companion. It suggests the fellowship or partnership of those who have common interests, common feelings, common work. It is a spiritual fellowship and has a double aspect, Godward as well as brotherward. It is the partnership of mutual Christian faith and life. It is upon Philemon's acceptance of this fellowship that Paul bases his appeal. The form of the conditional sentence assumes the reality of that fact. Philemon's refusal of Paul's request would be inconsistent with his acknowledgment of this partnership.

On this basis Philemon is urged to receive Onesimus as he would Paul. As a definite act Philemon is to receive Onesimus to himself (aorist middle). The heartiness of the reception desired for him is indicated by "as myself." "As" does not identify the persons but measures the warmth of the reception to be accorded him. "What joy would have entered the abode of Philemon, if the captive apostle had suddenly and unexpectedly stood before their eyes in the possession of his recovered liberty! Such a reception he now wishes that Onesimus may enjoy in the house of his master" (Van Oosterzee).

b. The promise of Paul, vv. 18, 19

The apostle at once takes care to remove a last hindrance which might arise in the mind of Philemon concerning the case. "If he hath wronged thee at all, or oweth thee aught, put that to mine account; I Paul write it with mine own hand, I will repay it." That Onesimus had done Philemon a definite injustice Paul grants by the form of his conditional sentence (first class). "Yet, the conditional form leaves it to Philemon to decide whether he, too, will consider that Onesimus did him a wrong and thus owes him the making good of that wrong" (Lenski). What the actual wrong was is only vaguely suggested by Paul in his words, "if he hath *wronged* thee at all, or *oweth* thee aught." The second verb defines more nearly the character of the wrong. Those expositors who lay special stress on the second verb conclude that Onesimus stole money from his master, either to enable him to flee, or stole and then fled to escape punishment. If this is the situation then Paul euphemistically describes the theft as a debt, thus sparing the penitent thief and avoiding irritation to Philemon.

Onesimus may have been guilty of theft as well as flight, but the words of Paul do not demand that interpretation. Admittedly Phrygian slaves had a very low reputation, yet this view may make the sin of Onesimus blacker than it really was. Would Paul have spoken of an immoral act like stealing in so hesitant a tone? If Onesimus had sinned in that way would not rather Paul have made an open acknowledgment of it and frankly asked Philemon for direct forgiveness? Would not such an open and unextenuated admission of the theft have been a nearer and surer way to the Christian heart of Philemon? If the injustice done is the theft of some money, then Paul makes no reference at all to the escape of Onesimus which must have been the primary offense.

It is quite probable that the clandestine escape of

Onesimus was itself the wrong which Paul has in mind. In that illegal flight "there was a wrong done to Philemon (in the shape of an affront to his honor, or a slur cast on his character as a master, which needed to be punished or pardoned), and there was damage or loss entailed by the bondman's absence from service, which needed to be refunded or repaired" (Drysdale). The escape was an act of injustice (if Philemon chose so to regard it) which Paul desired him wholly to overlook for his sake. But if Philemon felt that he should be indemnified for the loss which he had suffered, Paul obligates himself to repay it.

Onesimus cannot make the monetary restitution which Philemon might feel was his due, so Paul voluntarily assumes the debt incurred by him. As the spiritual father of Onesimus he assumes the obligation for him. It is a beautiful picture of what Christ on an infinitely higher plane has done for us all. As Luther remarked in his 1522 preface to the Epistle: "What Christ has done for us with God the Father, that St. Paul does for Onesimus with Philemon. . . . For we are all his Onesimi, if we believe."

To make binding his assumption of the obligation Paul writes: "I Paul write it with mine own hand, I will repay it." Thus Paul puts his signature on the bond to make it legal and binding. Some think that Paul here took the pen from the scribe and penned these lines himself. More probable is the view that he wrote the entire letter himself with his own hand. This would be unusual, for Paul usually dictated his letters to an amenuensis. It seems hardly probable that Paul would employ the services of a scribe for such a brief, friendly, and semiprivate letter. The composition of it with his own hand would be another indication to Philemon of the apostle's deep interest in the matter which called it forth.

Paul's promise to repay the debt of Onesimus is definite. "I will repay it." Discussions as to where Paul hoped to get the money to pay the obligation, should Philemon demand it, must not be used to cloud the sincerity of the apostle's promise to do so. The added words, "that I say not unto thee that thou owest to me even thine own self besides," are at times interpreted as though Paul is desirous of evading the full force of his promise just given, as if he were half retracting it and slyly suggesting that he did not really expect to pay it. We are told that Paul in a playful spirit calls Philemon's attention to the fact that he owes Paul a far greater debt than this, hence he cannot well expect Paul to pay this. This view is open to the objection that it makes Paul guilty of insincerity. Then Paul's offer was very largely a mere pretense. We cannot attribute such a view to Paul. When with his own hand Paul wrote that he would repay it, he meant just what he said. Should Philemon feel that he should be compensated for the loss sustained by him Paul would repay it. He found means to live during the years of his imprisonment and following his release he could earn the money by his own labors.

Paul's words are an instance of what is termed *paraleipsis*, "a construction in which the writer delicately protests against saying something which he nevertheless does say" (Vincent). Paul puts himself on record as assuming the obligation *in order to avoid* mentioning the great debt which Philemon owes him. Should Philemon require the fulfillment of it he pledges himself to honor it. But if Philemon should feel that he could not require it of the apostle, Paul shows him a way whereby such a remission of the payment may be fully justified on his part. Philemon owes Paul a double debt. "Thou owest to me even thine own self besides." Philemon owes his conversion to Paul, hence is debtor to him for all the spiritual wealth which has come to him. But this is "beside" the present debt he owes Paul for the return of his runaway slave who is now a vastly better slave than he was before.

c. The appeal to Philemon, v. 20

"Yes, brother," the apostle confesses, "I would like to make a profit off thee in the Lord!" (Lenski). The Greek is the aorist optative and expresses a wish rather than a command. His use of "brother" is indicative of his brotherly confidence in the one to whom it is expressed. "I" and "of thee" stand side by side in the original and are both emphatic. *Paul* desires a profit out of *Philemon*. For the moment he has identified himself with Onesimus; the desired reception of Onesimus will mean a profit for him. But the sphere of the profit is "in the Lord." For Paul it will not mean material gain but rather the spiritual benefit accruing from it for the Gospel. This act of brotherly love will bring an advantage to Paul in that it will make more widely and better understood the true nature and work of the Gospel of which he is now a messenger in bonds.

Having made known his wish, the apostle adds a direct appeal, "Refresh my heart in Christ." He begs Philemon to do for him what he has already done for the saints (v. 7). By a cordial reception of Onesimus he will give Paul courage and refreshment amid the limitations and discouragements of his imprisonment. The failure of Philemon to heed Paul's request would add further burdens to the apostle. It might have grave consequences for the furtherance of Christianity. It would seriously misrepresent the cause for which Paul labored and suffered; it would largely discredit the teaching of the Gospel and misrepresent its spirit before the world. But Philemon's Christian action in the case, so different from the customary action in such cases, would refresh the heart of Paul in that it furthered the cause of Christ.

d. The confidence of Paul, v. 21

Paul is confident that Philemon will not fail to make the desired response in this case. "Having confidence in thine obedience I write unto thee, knowing that thou wilt do even beyond what I say." It was this confidence in

Philemon's obedience which prompted him to write. He is sure that the claim of Christian duty as an appeal to his conscience will not go unheeded. Making use of the appeal of human expectancy, Paul is certain that Philemon will do even more than has been asked. It is always wise to anticipate good from God's people. It is a principle of great value which Christian leaders may well use with good effect in the furtherance of the cause of Christ.

Just what Paul meant by "beyond what I say" he left for the heart of his friend to decide. Does Paul imply that Philemon is to give Onesimus his freedom? He seems to have asked for almost everything short of this, so what else would he mean by this? Many commentators have concluded that Paul is hinting at the manumission of Onesimus. Others, however, reject such an inference and insist that it is merely a genial compliment to Philemon's character. If Paul does not hint that Onesimus be set free, he does ask something even harder, that Philemon receive and love him as a brother on a basis of spiritual equality with himself. Whatever Philemon understood Paul to imply by the statement, we can be sure that he was not slow in putting it into effect. Hackett well remarks: "The fact of our having this Epistle in our hands at the present moment is good proof that he was not remiss in acting up to every intimation of what was to be expected from his friendship or his love of justice; for our own feelings assure us that he would never have allowed such a letter to see the light, if it was to exist only as a perpetual witness of his ingratitude and his severity."

IV. THE CONCLUSION, vv. 22-25

But withal prepare me also a lodging: for I hope that through your prayers I shall be granted unto you. Epaphras, my fellow prisoner in Christ Jesus, saluteth thee: and so do Mark, Aristarchus, Demas, Luke, my fellow workers. The grace of our Lord Jesus Christ be with your spirit. Amen.

Paul concludes the Letter with a personal request in anticipation of his coming visit to Colossae (v. 22). This is followed by greetings from his companions (vv. 23-24) and the concluding benediction (v. 25).

1. The Personal Request, v. 22

To the appeal on behalf of Onesimus Paul adds a request for himself: "But withal prepare me also a lodging." Along with his granting of the request concerning Onesimus, Philemon will prepare for the coming visit of Paul. The tense of the verb is present and is consistent with the expectation of some delay. Paul asks that "a lodging" be prepared for him. The word may denote either "hospitality" or the "place of entertainment." Paul apparently uses it in the latter sense here since his unfailing modesty would not lead him to ask directly for Philemon's hospitality. The lodging may be either quarters in an inn or a room in a private house. Paul leaves the details to Philemon, but doubtless Philemon would arrange to lodge the apostle in his own home.

The import of this announcement is larger than a simple indication of an anticipated visit to Colossae. The announcement "would serve also indirectly to enforce Paul's application in behalf of Onesimus. Who could be willing to disappoint the beloved apostle, and compel him in person to see how little regard had been paid to his request?" (Van Oosterzee).

The reason for this request Paul indicates by adding: "For I hope that through your prayers I shall be granted unto you." The "your" is plural and marks a return to the plural of the salutation. Paul is certain of the prayers of all the Colossian saints on his behalf. Undoubtedly the prayers of Christians everywhere were centered on the apostle during his prolonged imprisonment. Paul conceived of the prayers of the saints as the instrument by which his deliverance might be brought about. Paul held that prayer had an objective as well as a subjective value.

He believed in prayer as a mighty working force in the spiritual universe. As such he sought and valued the prayers of others on his behalf, and he himself faithfully exercised such intercession for the saints.

He hopes soon to be granted his release as an act of grace or divine favor. This implies that Paul has received information that his case will soon receive a hearing by the imperial court. Later when writing to the Philippians he indicates that the trial is already in progress and that a verdict is expected soon. Paul also promised the Philippians a visit before very long (2:23-24).

In writing to the Romans some years before Paul indicated his plans about going on to Spain directly from Rome (Rom. 15:22-24). But the intervening years have modified his plans. The condition of affairs at Colossae and elsewhere has shown him the desirability of visiting his eastern churches before going on to the far west.

2. The Greetings from Friends, vv. 23, 24

Paul adds the names of five fellow Christians who join in sending greetings to Philemon personally. The list is identical to those sending greetings in the epistle to the Colossian church except that Jesus Justus is here omitted. This seems to imply that those here named were personally known to Philemon.

Epaphras is named first as being himself from Colossae and well known to Philemon. He was the founder of the Colossian church (Col. 1:7) but was now with Paul at Rome, whence he had gone to report to Paul the condition of affairs at Colossae (Col. 1:8; 4:12-13). Paul describes him as "my fellow prisoner in Christ Jesus." The title gives Philemon a last reminder of the apostle's imprisonment. "The significant addition, *in Christ Jesus,* keeps before us the truth, ever present to the mind of Paul, that this imprisonment stood in special relation to Christ" (Beet). Paul's designation of Epaphras has been understood to imply that Epaphras had also been imprisoned at Rome, perhaps because of his close relations to Paul. But since in Colossians 4:10 the term is applied to Aristarchus and withheld from Epaphras, although both epistles were written at the same time, it seems best to interpret it as meaning that these men voluntarily shared the apostle's confinement to minister to him. Thus the title is an expression of Paul's appreciation of their services to him.

The other four men are grouped under the designation, "my fellow workers." Paul gratefully recognizes them as engaged with him in the service of Christ. Mark is evidently John Mark, the writer of the second Gospel. From Colossians 4:10 we learn that he was expecting before long to go to Colossae where Paul bespeaks for him a warm welcome. Mark's former failure in service has been overcome and he has regained the confidence of Paul.

Aristarchus, a Macedonian (Acts 19:29), was one of Paul's close associates and made the trip to Rome with Paul (Acts 27:2). The name of Demas is honorably associated here with these other workers in Rome. But for Christians the name will ever carry a sad connotation, for during Paul's second imprisonment he deserted Paul, "having loved this present world" (II Tim. 4:10). The mention of Luke seems to imply that he was personally known to Philemon, although our knowledge of Luke as gleaned from hints in the Acts never associates him with the work in the Lycus valley. The name of Luke occurs only three times in the New Testament, yet he was a close and honored friend of the apostle. In Colossians Paul calls him, "Luke, the beloved physician" (4:14).

3. The Benediction, v. 25

The concluding benediction is similar in form and content to that used in Paul's other epistles. "The grace of our Lord Jesus Christ be with your spirit. Amen." "The grace of our Lord Jesus Christ" is invoked upon all the recipients of the letter. He began with a prayer for "grace and peace" upon them and closes with a prayer for the continuation of grace with them. By his use of "our" he makes the experience of this grace personal and included in it all the members of that great circle who receive "the Lord Jesus Christ" as their common Lord. That faith unites them in a common spiritual bond. And Christ Himself is to bestow His grace upon them.

As we look back upon the letter as it lies before us we are impressed anew with its unsurpassed beauty and charm. Its simple dignity, its refined Christian courtesy, its tactful consideration of others, its warm personal affection give ample proof of the quickening power of the Holy Spirit in the life and labors of the apostle Paul.

With the close of the Epistle the veil of history falls upon our knowledge of Philemon and Onesimus. We have no definite information as to the outcome of the letter, yet we need have no doubt as to what the actual outcome was. Paul himself appears to have had no doubt as to the outcome in the case. In Colossians 4:9 he refers to Onesimus as "the faithful and beloved brother, who is one of you." Since Onesimus would become a member of the church at Colossae, his warm description of him shows that he did not have any serious doubts as to the reception which Philemon would give his slave, now transformed by the grace of Christ.

Bibliography on Philemon

ALEXANDER, WILLIAM. "Philemon," *The Speaker's Commentary*, ed. F. C. COOK. London: John Murray, New Testament, Vol. III (1881), pp. 819-844.

BARNES, ALBERT. *Notes on the New Testament, Explanatory and Practical—Thessalonians, Timothy, Titus, and Philemon*, ed. ROBERT FREW. Grand Rapids: Baker Book House (1951 reprint), pp. 291-314.

BEET, JOSEPH AGAR. *A Commentary on St. Paul's Epistles to the Ephesians, Philippians, Colossians, and to Philemon*. London: Hodder and Stoughton (1890), pp. 255-269.

CHRYSOSTOM, S. JOHN. *The Homilies of S. John Chrysostom on the Epistles of St. Paul the Apostle to Timothy, Titus, and Philemon, Translated with Notes and Indices*. Oxford: John Henry Parker (1853), pp. 333-363.

DRYSDALE, A. H. "The Epistle of St. Paul to Philemon." *Devotional Commentary*. London: Religious Tract Society (1906 reprint), p. 186.

EALES, S. J. "The Epistle of Paul to Philemon," *The Pulpit Commentary*. Grand Rapids: Wm. B. Eerdmans Publishing Co. (1950 reprint), pp. xi and 19.

ERDMAN, CHARLES R. *The Epistles of Paul to the Colossians and to Philemon*. Philadelphia: The Westminster Press (1933), pp. 115-141.

HACKETT, see Van Oosterzee.

HARVEY, H. "Commentary on the Pastoral Epistles, First and Second Timothy and Titus; and the Epistle to Philemon," *An American Commentary on the New Testament*. Philadelphia: The American Baptist Publication Society (1890; reprint, no date), pp. 151-164.

LENSKI, R. C. H. *The Interpretation of St. Paul's Epistles to the Colossians, to the Thessalonians, to Timothy, to Titus, and to Philemon*. Columbus, Ohio: Lutheran Book Concern (1937), pp. 961-986.

LIGHTFOOT, J. B. *Saint Paul's Epistles to the Colossians and to Philemon*. London: Macmillan & Co. (1927 reprint), pp. 299-344.

MACLAREN, ALEXANDER. "The Epistles of St. Paul to the Colossians and to Philemon," *The Expositor's Bible*. Grand Rapids: Wm. B. Eerdmans Publishing Co. (1943 reprint), Vol. VI, pp. 291-309.

MEYER, HEINRICH AUGUST WILHELM. *Critical and Exegetical Hand-Book to the Epistles to the Philippians and Colossians, and to Philemon*. New York: Funk & Wagnalls Company (1885), pp. 395-420.

MOULE, H. C. G. "The Epistles of Paul the Apostle to the Colossians and to Philemon," *Cambridge Bible for Schools*. Cambridge: University Press (1932 reprint), pp. 145-178.

VINCENT, MARVIN R. *A Critical and Exegetical Commentary on the Epistle to the Philippians and to Philemon*. (*I.C.C.*) Edinburgh: T. & T. Clark (1950 reprint), pp. 157-194.

VAN OOSTERZEE, J. J. "The Epistle of Paul to Philemon," Lange's *Commentary on The Holy Scriptures—Thessalonians, Timothy, Titus, Philemon, Hebrews*. Translated from the German with additions by DR. HACKETT. Grand Rapids: Zondervan Publishing House (1950 reprint), p. 31.

WILLIAMS, A. LUKYN. "The Epistles of Paul the Apostle to the Colossians and to Philemon," *Cambridge Greek Testament*. Cambridge: University Press (1928 reprint), pp. lxvi-lxxiv and 172-191.